FAMILY ARCHAEOLOGY

✳

Discovering the Family Skeleton and Making It Dance

Freya Ottem Hanson

HERITAGE BOOKS
2012

HERITAGE BOOKS
AN IMPRINT OF HERITAGE BOOKS, INC.

Books, CDs, and more—Worldwide

For our listing of thousands of titles see our website
at
www.HeritageBooks.com

Published 2012 by
HERITAGE BOOKS, INC.
Publishing Division
100 Railroad Ave. #104
Westminster, Maryland 21157

International Standard Book Numbers
Paperbound: 978-0-7884-2264-5
Clothbound: 978-0-7884-9460-4

This book is dedicated
to my
Aunt Freeda and Uncle Arno

❤

Thank you for all the prayers and
encouragement

TABLE OF CONTENTS

FORWARD

———

Your kind of folk

Each time he came to baby-sit, Iver Watten would place a bag filled with candy bars on the corner of the dining room table. Since we rarely got candy, my brothers and I were convinced that Iver must be one of the wealthiest people in the world. Ironically, he was orphaned, grew up in my grandparents' home in North Dakota, and died penniless.

People influence us, even babysitters who patiently read books to restless children. Parents, brothers, sisters, grandparents, aunts, uncles, and cousins all shape our lives. Even pastors, teachers, neighbors, scout leaders, 4-H leaders, and soccer coaches leave their imprints on us and become part of the fabric of our family story.

People make history interesting. When you look at members of your family, you just might be taking a good look at yourself. Take another look at that family portrait. You may have grown pleasingly accustomed to those faces. After all they are your kind of folk.

CREATING A LEGACY

Blending old and new

New Orleans, blends the new with the old to make this one of the most fascinating metro acres in the world. The charm of the old city surrounding Jackson Square and the a new modern city of skyscrapers stand side-by-side. Families also have interesting blends of old and new, both of which need to be treasured and cherished. This book suggests ways to discover hidden treasure from the past and to create new. More than writing down old memories, you will be challenged to create and shape new ones.

This book will encourage you to learn more about the people in your family. You will rediscover family values, traditions, and stories, and by doing so you will experience your heritage in a way that gives flight to new stories. Whether you revisit a school, church, take a trip with a child to a foreign country, or trace information on your ancestors, learning more about your family can help you better understand yourself.

On the grounds of Mount Vernon, animals graze and abundant gardens grow recreating a scene similar to the days when our first President occupied this grand estate. But living history is not just for the wealthy or the curators of museums. All of us can recreate our own history. Whether you stroll down a country road where your grandfather walked, or wind up his watch that you inherited, or visit the church where you were baptized, all of these experiences give way to retelling your history and weaving a rich family tapestry or others to enjoy. Rather than concentrating on the information you don't have, begin with what you have, and then see what new treasure can come out of this rich family storehouse.

The Bible in Matthew 13:52 describes the ready scribe as one *"who is like the master of a household who brings out of his treasure what is new and what is old."* So look for the old, but don't stop there. Bring out new stories and create a living history.

Freya Otttem Hanson

GETTING STARTED

Taking another look at your family

A professional producer of family videos said, "All families are good looking." I often think about his comment when I glance through family photo albums, and notice the unique blending of physical characteristics in a family.

Families also make for interesting research. This book will give you an opportunity to discover who you are and the people you call family. You may wonder where to begin to find these stories and memories. I would suggest you start with your immediate family, and then move back to your parents and then to your siblings. Then step back yet another generation to your grandparents. While you search the archives of your life, look for fresh ways to incorporate that new data you discover into your life. Figuratively, get out the dust rag and the Old English polish, and begin with some of these sources of information:

PHOTO ALBUMS

When asked what you would remove from a burning home, you might respond, "The family photo albums." Pictures are a powerful visual memory of times past. My mother willed me her photo albums, but neither she nor I realized that my brothers would also want those pictures. Thank goodness duplicates of pictures can be made to satisfy family members. The

1

investment is small in comparison to hurt feelings.

As I looked through those albums, I couldn't help but chuckle when I recalled how my mother would rip up photos that were unflattering of her before putting them in the album.

LETTERS

Letters open up windows to the past. Because letters weren't written for publication, often they tell a more honest story. Letters are a priceless source for learning about people, their feelings, their sorrows, their hopes, and their disappointments. My father wrote letters to his mother while he was in World War II. I compiled those letters because of the unique story they told. My father also wrote letters to my son on the anniversary of his baptism. Those letters to his grandson can encourage, even though my father is no longer alive to do so.

INTERVIEWS

Each generation has its own treasured stories. Make sure you write them down before they escape forever. You may want to use a tape recorder to record information or take notes on eavesdropped conversations. Be prepared to ask questions, and jot down any information of value. I learned from my father that his father was quite vain and showed great concern over a receding hairline. Now when I stare in a mirror at times and think I have more wrinkles than I should, I smile and I think of my grandfather's vanity.

CHURCH RECORDS

Church records can include birth, baptismal, confirmation, marriage and even death information on parishioners. My father researched his roots back to the 1500s through the use of church records in Norway. Visit churches where family members worshiped. Often times church records include vital statistics and pictures that can be invaluable to you.

PUBLIC RECORDS

Offices of vital statistics, usually located in your county seat, maintain extensive records on births, marriages and deaths. Certified copies can be obtained at a nominal cost, however, you may need to know approximate dates in order to eliminate frustrating and painstaking searches.

NEWSPAPER ARTICLES

"A good time was had by all." Check your local newspaper for information on births, weddings, deaths, and other social news. Newspapers remain a staple for family news, especially small town or suburban newspapers that are more likely to include personal family stories.

The *"Black Hills Pioneer"* newspaper recently featured my aunt from Spearfish, South Dakota. She was one of two patrons who owned a library card dating back to 1946, the year the public library opened in her hometown. That small article provided interesting family information.

SCHOOL BOOKS

School yearbooks contain important facts about family members. Besides school photos, such books often include school activities and achievements. You might even be able to recall teachers, whose names you have forgotten.

SCRAPBOOKS

Scrapbooks allow us a glimpse of life at a specific time. I made a scrapbook of a family trip to Winnipeg, Manitoba to see Queen Elizabeth II. That book chronicles a ten-year-old girl's memory of this event. Be careful when opening the pages of a scrapbook, however, a dried prom corsage might crumble out.

AUTOGRAPH BOOKS

I picked up the autograph book of my great grandmother only to be amazed at the beautiful verses these young women wrote in the late 1800s. I also marveled at their impeccable cursive penmanship. Autograph books tell the story of friendships. Enjoy them. Consider leaving one out for your guests to sign.

MILITARY RECORDS

If you are a next of kin, you can obtain a relative's military records. Although some people succeed in getting valuable reports through this source, when I attempted to obtain my father's World War II military records, I met disappointment. Fire had destroyed his files, and the only remaining document was his honorable discharge, a copy of which I already had.

ORGANIZATIONAL RECORDS

Many organizations maintain membership lists and other information about their work. If a family member belonged to an organization, you may want to check with the secretary to see if a history was kept. If the organization seems reluctant to release information, they may be willing to do so if they know the purpose of your search.

BABY BOOKS

My mother kept a detailed baby book of my early years. Inside that pink, satin covered book entitled, *"All her Life"* there is a lock of hair, foot and hand prints, weight and height charts, and family photos that range from my first birthday to my wedding day. Baby books usually have pages for photos

Family Archaeology

and other vital information such as medical records and school data. In my own book, my mother diligently recorded the dates I lost each baby tooth and when the permanent one appeared.

JOURNALS AND DIARIES

For over thirty years my father kept a daily journal of the activities on the North Dakota farm where he was born in 1907. He first recorded details about the weather, when each field was planted, and when those fields were harvested. Later he began to include more information in his journal. After my father died, my mother continued the project, and wrote in the loose-leaf notebook up to November 24, 1996, the day before her death. Journals and diaries record daily family life, with all its joys and sorrows.

FAMILY REUNIONS

Nothing quite matches a family reunion for gathering stories and information about your kinfolk. Don't neglect this source before it is too late. You can encourage someone else to plan it, but if no one rises to the task, consider taking it on. The family memories you hear will make it worthwhile.

The key with all family memories is to begin with what you have. Even if you don't possess scrapbooks or journals or newspaper clippings, your own stories will provide a springboard for discussion. You may be pleasantly surprised to discover that when you put one piece in place more will also fit. The family tapestry will grow, and instead of finding your family story ordinary, you will find stories worth remembering. Trust me. I know. For now . . . happy searching.

ONE
THE SKELETON IN THE CLOSET

Searching for relative information and how to begin

George Bernard Shaw said, "If you can't get rid of the family skeleton, you may as well make it dance." Has anyone in your family prepared a genealogy? Recently my aunt gave me the family tree of my great grandfather, Vincent Samuel Jansa. Born in 1858 in Landskron, Bohemia, he died at ninety-one in Spearfish, South Dakota. I looked at the names of eight generations of Jansa that had preceded him. All were from Landskron, Bohemia. He was the first in his family to come to America, and he was also the first in his family to leave the Roman Catholic Church. What bold steps those must have been for him.

A distant cousin traveled to Landskron and compiled the list of these ancestors of mine back to 1550. Had he not taken those painstaking efforts, I would not have known my ties to Mikulas, Nikodem, Vaclav, Pavel, Jan, Joseph, and Vincent or Maruse, Zuzana, Marina, Josefina and Olxbila. These names in my genealogy give me a sense of connectedness to the past.

LET'S TALK

1. Has anyone in your family done family research? What was the result?

7

2. Discuss the importance of having a family tree. Have you received a family tree? What does it say about your genealogy?

LET'S DISCOVER

1. Look for family trees in Bibles, baby books, or other family records. What do they say about your family?
2. Check the names, dates of birth and death of relatives. What did you learn?
3. If adopted, how do you relate to a family tree?
4. What stories have you been told about your ancestors? Which were funny and which were sad? Have any of those stories been written down?
5. Take a look at photos of ancestors? What similarities exist between family members?

LET'S PLAN

1. Make a diagram with names, dates, and places of birth and death of your ancestors. Fill in the information you have, and don't worry about missing data. You can fill in information as it becomes known.
2. Plan a trip to a foreign country to begin research about your family.
3. Before you depart, ask others in your family what they know about your foreign connections. These conversations could save you hours of fruitless searching.
4. Write down family stories you have been told. Another generation will appreciate knowing if a great grandfather was a fisherman or if someone in your family turned down a royal title to marry your great grandmother.
5. Use a computer genealogy program to make an attractive family tree. Consider giving your efforts as a Christmas present. Even if you can't find out about the past, a few phone calls will help you make a family tree that includes the present. Family members will appreciate having the dates of birth of the current generation, and might find it handy when planning inheritances or remembering birthdays.

6. Are there hidden stories about your family? Why might those tales be embarrassing? Who was privy to them and from whom were those stories hidden?

7. From what countries did your ancestors come? How did their "homeland" influence them? My husband's Finnish relatives, for example, went to great lengths to preserve the tradition of the sauna.

The Old Testament records many genealogies. Look in both Genesis and Chronicles. Yet, other than Jesus' genealogy found in Matthew and Luke, the New Testament is notably absent of such lists. We don't even know the genealogies of Matthew, Mark, Luke or John. Possibly the point is well taken, that even though you may have a wonderful genealogy, it is not the end all and be all. Who your ancestors are is important, but not as important as what you become.

TWO
PRIDE AND PREJUDICE

Learning about nationality and other ethnic ties

Where did your ancestors come from? What were they like? What was their nationality? Whatever your nationality, we all have one, even if that means calling yourself a "true blooded American."

Learning about ancestors can be fun, and nationality can impact how we talk, the color of our hair and eyes, and even how long we might live.

My father and I took a trip to Norway in 1980. That journey was significant because 100 years prior to that time my grandfather had left Norway for America. Now we were returning to his place of birth. We met relatives and visited my grandparent's home site where he lived prior to coming to this country in the 1880s. I especially remember the visit to his birth home. Relatives, dressed in native costumes, greeted and welcomed us as though we were royalty. I kept thinking they must have been expecting someone else until it dawned on me that we were the ones being so honored. Their hospitality left me in awe of a kind and generous people who pulled out the red carpet for folks such as we.

11

LET'S TALK

1. What is your national background? Who were your ancestors?
2. Who in your family knows about these people? Would you like to talk with them? Think of questions you might like to ask them.
3. Are there physical likenesses in your family members? Who do you look like?
4. When did your ancestors come to America? Why did they make that journey?
5. Identify some prominent characteristics of people of your nationality? For example are they fair skinned or do they have darker complexions? Are they quiet and hardworking who stick to themselves or do they prefer to get together for a party and will do so at the drop of a hat?
6. How do you fit the mold? Or have you broken it?

LET'S DISCOVER

1. Locate pictures of your parents, grandparents and even grandparents. Identify the people in the pictures and then make certain their names and any other information you might have about them are recorded on the back. Don't worry about your handwriting.
2. Find a recording of the national anthem of an ancestor's country. if possible attempt to learn it. You might even find it readily available on a CD.
3. Listen to a language tape or CD from an ancestor's country of origin. Can you say hello and good-bye in that language? You may want to take a language course or rent or purchase languages tapes in order to acquaint yourself with a few words, or you can purchase a language book in a bookstore and practice some of the more common phrases.
4. Check out cultural societies that exist to promote the heritage and customs of your country of origin. Consider membership.
5. Look over cookbooks from foreign countries. Plan a cook and taste party.

Family Archaeology

You may want to invite friends and relatives and hold a cooking party. Make notes on what tasted good, and don't forget to laugh over the goofs.

LET'S PLAN

1. Find about relatives in a foreign country. Make contact with them. The phrase book will help you write a few lines of introduction.
2. Take a trip with a relative to the country of your ancestors. Even if you can't make contact with relatives there, seeing the places and hearing the language will help you reconnect with the rich heritage you share in common.
3. Purchase a flag of your country of origin and fly it on special days. Write down what you learned about your ancestral national background. That information will give you a greater understanding of your heritage. You may want to share what you learned with relatives or friends.

It's easy to get caught up in national pride. I live in an Irish town and March 17th looks like a national holiday here. It's also a good time to run for cover. For certain, the Irish love a great party and their unique humor gives way to wondrous laughter right here in St. Paul, Minnesota.

THREE
WHAT'S YOUR JOHN HENRY?

Discovering the importance of your name

O ne of the first things we learn in life is our name, and then we learn to write it. Once when my two brothers were very small, presumably two or three years of age, someone in the town asked them their names. My eldest brother puffed out his chest and exploded with his full name, "I am Charles Iver Ottem." Then my younger brother, Jack, said, "I'm baby Yatzy."

Our names give us a definition and many of those names come from a national or familial background. When I was born, my father named me "Freya" after the Norwegian goddess of love and beauty. Being 100% Norse, my father prided himself in giving me a unique Scandinavian name. So when my son was born, we didn't hesitate to give him the name John Jacob Hanson IV. His father, his grandfather, and his great-grandfather had all shared in that namesake.

Women often change their names based on marital status, and immigrants have been known to Americanize a difficult foreign name. My husband's Finnish ancestors changed their surname from "Niemi" to the common "Hanson" name. Names are important.

Family Archaeology

LET'S TALK

1. Talk about changes in names that occurred when your relatives came to this country. For example, my Norwegian grandmother changed the spelling of her Norwegian name, "Kari" to read "Carrie."
2. Discuss the origins of your surname.
3. What prompted your parents to give you your first name?
4. If you have changed your name, talk about your reaction to that change. Recently at a high school reunion it was fun to be known by my maiden name again .
5. Who gave you your middle name? Is there a story or some history behind it?
6. Find out what family member's names mean. A baby book of names can help you.
7. Do you have a nickname? Who gave it to you? What is your reaction? I learned to my surprise that my niece didn't mind her nickname "pumpkin seed." It could be because a favorite uncle gave it to her.
8. If you could use a pen name, what would it be?

LET'S PLAN

1. List first names that appear in your family tree. Are they ethnic in background?
2. Make a list of surnames that appear in your maternal ancestral line? Note any of interest.
3. Ask your parents what you were called before you were born? When I was pregnant, we called our unborn child (we didn't know the sex in those days) ToivoLena. These were Finnish names. Toivo was a boy's name and Lena a girl's name.
4. What mix-ups have you encountered because of your name? Possibly you have gotten a bad credit report or an obnoxious phone call because someone else also shares your name.

The Israelites spent considerable time naming a child. The name Isaac meant *"laughter."* Sarah, who had long given up hope of having a child, laughed when she was told in a year she would be the mother of a son. After an important encounter with God, Jacob's name became *"Israel,"* a name synonymous with the modern State of Israel.

A name gives us identity. A good name, according to Proverbs 3:3-4, is more valuable than riches. Treasure your name and make good on it.

FOUR
PILGRIM'S PROGRESS

Taking note of religious preferences

The Pilgrims landed at Plymouth Bay, Massachusetts on Christmas Day, 1620. Among those early arrivals were a group of separatists known as Puritans. Unable to reform the Church of England, this strident group separated from the "mother church" and formed its own congregations, which were branded illegal. Eventually this band of Christians fled England first for Amsterdam and then came to America but not without leaving their mark..

In England they supported laws that closed the theaters and prohibited the sale of liquor. As might be expected, they held a healthy distrust of anything called monarchy, and supported freedom of religion and the right to assemble. No wonder those basic foundational beliefs were included in the First Amendment to the U.S. Constitution and so deeply embedded in American religious and political thought.

These immigrants also held strong beliefs about prayer, Bible reading and Christian virtue. Following the teachings of John Calvin and John Wycliffe, they eventually became known as Congregationalists because they held a strong belief that the congregation, and not a large church body,

19

should be in charge of the life of believers.

My mother was raised in that belief system. A morally upright woman with the highest of virtues, she joined my father's denomination when they married, but her views of life, how she lived, and how she parented were deeply rooted in the beliefs she had been taught as a child.

What religious views have shaped your life? Take time to find out.

"Many who quarrel about religion never practice it." Benjamin Franklin claimed. He thought his church only wanted converts and was not interested in relating to the world. As a result, Franklin left his denomination and practiced a private faith. He wrote about this decision in his autobiography, "I went no more to the public assemblies."

Possibly there are some in your family who left the church of their parents. I am told that my great grandfather left his childhood church because an elder boxed him on the ears. I've often wondered what he did to deserve that kind of treatment or even if the story is true.

LET'S TALK

1. Describe your religious upbringing. In what religion were you raised? Was this the religion of either of your parents?

2. What specific religious rituals did you practice in your home? Were there mealtime or bedtime prayers or readings from a religious book?

3. What religious instruction were you given as a child? Where was this teaching given and who was in charge? How did it influence you?

4. Do you recall a particularly meaningful religious experience as a child? Think about a first communion or a confirmation or a time at a Bible camp.

5. What leadership positions in your church or synagogue did your parents or grandparents hold? My grandfather was a "founding father" of the church I attended as a child.

6. What positions have you held in your church or synagogue? What did you enjoy about that role. What difficulties did the position present?

7. What do you like about your church? What could be improved?

8. How have your parents influenced and shaped your religious views? Which views have you rejected?

LET'S DISCOVER

1. What are the specific beliefs that your particular church or synagogue holds? How do those differ from other denominations? If you do not know, talk to a leader in your congregation, the minister, or consult a reference book on various faiths.
2. What sacraments, ceremonies, or rites (such as baptism, confirmation, holy communion, bar mitzvah) does your religion celebrate? If you or a close family member has been involved in such a rite, describe its importance to a friend, family member, or a young person of your faith.
3. What religious tensions exist in your family? How have they been resolved or do they remain "troubled waters?" Have family ties been cut-off because someone married outside the faith?
4. Has anyone in your family pursued a career as a pastor or church worker? Ask them about that experience. Did the family or the church support that decision?
5. Do you know of family or friends who worship in a house church?
6. Research your denomination's history. What fascinates you about your church's founding?
7. Tell another person how important your faith is to you. You may want to speak with a child or grandchild or a young person in your church

LET'S PLAN

1. Write down a statement of your faith and place it with other important papers. Your children may appreciate your words.
2. Remember significant religious events in your life. Note them on a calendar.
3. Celebrate religious holidays in your church or synagogue.
4. If you are a Christian, attend a Christmas Eve service or Good Friday or Easter service. If you are Jewish, attend the high Jewish festivals of

Yom Kippur and Rosh Hashanah.

5. What is your favorite religious holiday? What makes it meaningful for you?

The following are the five major religions in the world, Christian, Islam, Hindu, Buddhist, and Judaism. Did you know that nearly 81% of the world's population has some kind of religion? There are two billion Christians in 260 countries, 1.3 billion Muslims in 184 countries, and 15 million Jews in 134 countries.

FIVE

I HEREBY DECLARE, ON OATH

———

Finding out about citizenship and what it means

The Canadian custom's officer asked us at Niagara Falls, *"Are you folks United States citizens?"* As he peeped into our car, we all nodded our heads in agreement.

"How long do you intend to be in Canada?" he asked.

"Just long enough to see the falls – an hour or so."

On our return trip we faced a United States custom's officer. All he seemed concerned about was how much we had spent in Canada, and then he asked if we were all United States citizens. My husband, our fifteen-year-old son, and I all nodded in agreement.

Citizenship gives a person an identity – a homeland with which to be connected. The idea of citizenship came from the ancient Greeks as far back as 700 BC. A person was a member of a city (spawning the word "citizenship") and not necessarily a nation. Socrates who lived from 469 – 399 BC must have scoffed such a limited view of citizenship, and boldly announced, *"I am not an Athenian or a Greek but a citizen of the world."*

The Romans expanded the rights of their citizens to include privileges throughout the entire Roman Empire. A Roman citizenship was coveted and not to be taken lightly. The Apostle Paul, a Roman citizen, used the privileges of citizenship to advance the Christian faith during the first century.

In America, we understand citizenship to be either by jus soli (the right of soil) or by jus sanguinis (the right of blood) while others come to citizenship through a process called naturalization. Naturalization involves meeting residency and language requirements, and also passing an examination on American government. The group swearing-in process takes place in a specially designated place, usually a court of law, where the inductee swears to uphold the laws of the United States and denounce foreign citizenship in these words:

"I hereby declare, on oath, that I absolutely and entirely renounce and abjure all allegiance and fidelity to any foreign prince, potentate state, or sovereignty of which or which I have hereto before been a subject or citizen; that I will support and defend the Constitution and the laws of the United States of America against all enemies, foreign and domestic; that I will bear true faith and allegiance to the same . . . and that I take this obligation freely without any mental reservation of purpose of evasion; so help me God."

A Canadian born friend of mine who married a U.S. citizen, confessed that when she became naturalized she understood the words she was expected to say, but found it difficult to denounce her beloved Canada and simply mouthed some of them.

LET'S TALK

1. Which of your ancestors became U.S. citizens?
2. What process did they undergo to become citizens?
3. What were the requirements for citizenship?
4. How did you become a United States citizen? (naturalization, by birth, or by blood)
5. What privileges do you have because you are a United States citizen? Do you give those rights much thought? For example, think about the right to own land, vote, hold public office, and enjoy the freedoms

outlined in the Bill of Rights to the Constitution.

LET'S DISCOVER

1. Try to locate naturalization papers for someone in your family. What does the Certificate of Naturalization say? My husband's grandfather's naturalization certificate has information about his age, height, race, complexion, color of eyes and hair. The names of his wife and minor children are also included on the certificate. Although he was 100% Finnish, the certificate showed that he was a subject of Russia because Russia controlled Finland at the time of his immigration. The certificate also stated that "Victor Huikko had resided continuously in the United States for at least five years and in Minnesota for at least one year." The seal of the court not only declared the date the "2nd day of December in the year of our Lord nineteen hundred eighteen" but it also added that it was "the year of our Independence the one hundred and forty-third."

2. From what country did your ancestors come? What prompted them to come to this country?

3. What privileges did your ancestors enjoy because they came to America? My grandfather for example, received 160 acres of farmland in North Dakota, a gift of the government.

4. Has any family member had dual citizenship? When did they make a choice which citizenship to claim?

5. Do you know of anyone who gave up citizenship in the USA to live in another country? What were the reasons?

LET'S PLAN

1. Plan to watch a naturalization ceremony. Events like this take place on Citizenship Day, which is September 17. Call the Bureau of Immigration and Naturalization in your area for more information.

2. Find out where you might be able to locate naturalization papers on ancestors. Make photocopies of those documents and place them in album.

3. Let someone know how proud you are to be an American. Fly the American flag on June 14th, Flag Day, the Fourth of July, Presidents' Day or Veterans Day. Attend a Memorial Day program that honors those who gave their lives for this country. Did you fly a flag as a symbol of solidarity and unity in the days and weeks following the collapse of the World Trade Center? What did that mean for you?

I remember how overwhelmed and teary-eyed I became when our plane landed on United States soil. The event was over thirty years ago and after five weeks overseas for the first time in my life, I was returning home – home to my own beloved USA. It took a foreign visit for me to hold my U.S. passport ever so closely as I waited in line with my luggage until it was my turn to proceed through customs. As I stood in that airport, I wondered what emotions my grandparents must have felt when they came to America for the first time in the 1880s, a land they too would declare their beloved USA.

SIX
SO YOU WENT TO HARVARD?

Studying up on educational pursuits in your family

The American writer, Mark Twain said, *"I have never let my schooling interfere with my education."* Even though it has been said that a cauliflower is a cabbage with a college education, we know that a law degree from Harvard speaks louder on Wall Street than one from a Midwestern university. That Harvard degree has long bought a bigger salary and a longer commute.

Since I was a young girl, I knew my parents expected me to go to college. My parents had attended college in the 1920's and 1930's, when a high school diploma meant you were well educated. As a result they had specific educational expectations for each of us children and laid them out for us. Although we children all acquired post secondary education, I've learned that education is more than degrees, and most often occurs when we aren't buried in a textbook.

It has been said that Moses, one of the greatest leaders of all time, received three educations. The first from his mother; the second from Pharaoh's Egyptian courts; and the third from the wilderness of the Sinai where he was educated in the school of "hard knocks." From which school have you learned the most? Keep your eyes open, you may have an

27

educational opportunity today that no Harvard graduate could receive. Don't miss it.

LET'S TALK

1. Where did you attend school? What do your recall about the time you spent in elementary school, high school, college, or postgraduate school?
2. What did the building or buildings look like?
3. Did you choose to attend these schools or was it more by proximity?
4. What subjects did you study in each of them?
5. Which subjects did you like?
6. Did you get a degree or participate in an activity because your parents wanted you to?
7. What memorable high school experience still gives you a smile?
8. What teacher influenced you the most? In what way? Have you considered writing and thanking that teacher?
9. What teacher did you dislike? How did that affect you? Did it change your outlook on a certain subject?
10. What was the attitude of your family about education? Something to be endured or was it something to be enjoyed?
11. How has your education affected what you do?

LET'S DISCOVER

1. What schooling did your parents receive? How did that influence your choices?
2. Look at your school yearbooks. Tell someone (maybe a child or niece or nephew) about your friends, your activities, and what was going on in the world at that time.
3. What nontraditional educational experiences have you received? Think about travel seminars, Elder hostel programs, or continuing education classes.

4. Name a school of "hard knocks" you attended. For example, think about a business or personal venture that taught you more than any MBA degree.

5. What lessons have you learned, either in a traditional or nontraditional educational setting that you might like to pass on to your children or a young person. Consider mentoring a young person.

6. What continuing education or relicensure does your career require? How do you react to those requirements?

LET'S PLAN

1. Plan to visit schools you attended as a child. Observe how they have changed. Recently I participated in the closure of the elementary and high school I attended as a youth. The small, rural North Dakota town could no longer muster up enough students to justify a school, so the district voted to close the school. Over 600 graduates and friends of the school came to the reunion, where hands were held in a human chain that surrounded the old school building. As hands were clasped, the school bell tolled eighty-five times, once for each year the school had been in session. As we looked at the tired and worn 1916 building, it helped to recall the description of one of the oldest graduates present. Now 85 his memories went back to that building when he was a young boy. To him the structure was "wonderful." Inside those walls was indoor plumbing and warm showers, state of the art, something most of the homes in the area lacked. Regardless of the condition of your school, I would encourage you to simply call it "wonderful."

2. Get together with a school chum and talk about the good old school days. Take along your yearbooks. They will help generate memories.

3. Plan or attend a class reunion, even if you are 20 pounds heavier than you were way back then.

4. Write a letter or call a classmate.

5. Collect school pictures and put them in a special album.

6. Think about educational experiences you would like to have. Plan how you might get that education in the next year or even four. Think about computer, mechanics, home repairs, or even finishing college degree.

Francis Keppel said, *"Education is too important to be left solely to the educators."* We are all educators whether we realize it or not, and we are all students too. Parents teach such indelible habits in their children that generations can't unlearn them. A teacher's influence never ends.

SEVEN
WHEN YOU GROW UP

Discovering career choices in your family

A t my husband John's 25th high school reunion, one of the teachers showed my husband an index card on which his name and future ambitions were recorded. My husband had filled that card out twenty-five years before. These words were written after the line entitled, "future ambitions:" "Does not know what he wants to do."

"That hasn't changed much," my husband said. "I'm still wondering what I will do when I grow up." Many of us struggle with the idea of a career, and in today's workplace; job choices can make that decision even more confusing.

Growing up, I envisioned myself working as a journalist like Barbara Walters. Then my career ambitions shifted to being a criminal trial lawyer like F. Lee Bailey, and while in college, I became fascinated with the nonviolent peace work of Mohandas Gandhi and Martin Luther King, Jr. In many ways, however, how I would carry out my career was influenced by my mother. After attending law school and having a family, I decided to practice law out of my home. My mother ran an insurance company out of her home. So I set up a business with the most obvious role model in mind – my own mother.

Likewise, we may not choose a career as much as it may choose us. My

31

brothers continue a third generation of family farming on the same homestead my grandfather claimed in 1882. Besides farmers, my family has many teachers. It shouldn't have surprised me when I married into a family where teaching was valued. And I too have sought opportunities to teach. Often when it comes to our work, we choose the familiar. Ralph Waldo Emerson said, *"I look on that man as happy, who, when there is a question of success, looks into his work for a reply."*

LET'S TALK

1. Describe your work. Think about the daily tasks, the responsibility, the expertise needed, and the satisfaction and dissatisfaction your work gives you.
2. Why did you choose your particular career? Do others in your family share the same interests?
3. What educational requirements were needed for your job? Did you go through a separate examination in order to qualify?
4. What work have family members done? Think about your grandparents, parents, aunts, uncles, siblings, and even your children. Any similarities? Do some work in a common business venture? What tensions does that give occasion for?
5. What types of work have women done in your family? I was the first woman in my family to become a lawyer, but I have many aunts who were career women. Several were teachers and others were nurses. One sold real estate. Discuss attitudes family members hold about working women.

LET'S DISCOVER

1. Describe your first job, even if it was scooping ice cream at the local Bridgeman's ice cream parlor. Recall your pay. What lessons about work did you learn from that experience?
2. What is the most exciting job assignment you have had? I still fondly recall working as a senate intern in Washington DC one summer while

I was in college. It remains for me one of my interesting work assignments.

3. What effect did a job or career change have on your family? What caused the need to change? Think about office politics, promotions, downsizing, and layoffs.

4. What workaholic behaviors, if any, have you noticed in yourself or others in your family? How do those work habits affect family members?

LET'S PLAN

1. Choose five careers you wish you had pursued. Talk about them with a close family member. Consider what makes that career interesting to you. Plan to introduce a taste of that career into your life. For example if you have wanted to be an actress, consider volunteering as a walk-on in a community play. Or if you always wanted to build houses, volunteer on a Habitat for Humanity project.

2. Take a career assessment test and learn what careers fit your interests and abilities. Introduce parts of those jobs into your life. For example, if you can't be a plumber, you can still learn how to fix your own. I'm sure family members will welcome your help too.

3. What career advice would you give a young person today?

4. If you want a career change, explore options. One mother, who couldn't sleep until her teenage son came home, began a career as a poet. See the potential of turning an otherwise negative experience into a positive one.

5. What would your ideal job be? Think about working hours, flexibility, benefits, projects, earnings, and stress. What parts of that ideal job are already present in your current work?

6. If you are unhappy with your present work, write down five things you can do to begin the process of changing your work or improving your attitude about the job you have. For example, as a lawyer I decided to no longer do divorce work after having been engaged in that practice for

twenty-five years. Such a decision takes time. It took over a year to conclude the divorce files I had.

Kahil Gibran once said, *"Work is love made visible."* As much as we may enjoy weekends, vacation or even dream of retirement, endless vacations may not provide as much enjoyment as we may think. A great joy is to love your work. God gave Adam the task of taking care of the Garden of Eden long before the fall. Rather than a curse, work is meant to be a blessing and delight. So may you find yourself singing happily: "Off to work I go."

EIGHT
MILITARY MEMORIES

Tracking down military experiences

Whether you tap your toes to *"Anchors Aweigh my Boys,"* or *"From the Halls of Montezuma,"* or *"Over Hill, Over Dale, As we Hit the Dusty Trail,"* each of those songs has a common thread – the military.

Each Memorial Day when I was a young child, I heard patriotic speeches, listened to *"God Bless America"* and heard the chilling sound of taps played over the graves of war veterans. The men and women from the local unit of the American Legion proudly displayed flags and came to the town hall for a program. One woman, a gold star mother, was ushered into the hall and given a seat of prominence for the program. I learned that she had lost a son in World War I. As a young child, I recall thinking, "What a sacrifice that woman made." After the morning program, a caravan of townsfolk accompanied the color guard to the neighboring cemetery where rifles were fired over the graves of those who had served their country. This farming community paused from their spring work to commemorate the solemn reality of what freedom can cost a nation.

Recently I learned from my brother, who heads up the American Legion Post in Osnabrock, North Dakota, that our father had given him some advice many years ago. He had told my brother, "Memorial Day never comes at the right time in a farming community. All of us want to be in the fields, but one-half a day is not too much to ask for this noble cause." My brother never forgot those words and recently gave tribute to those words at a gathering of Osnabrock people.

Military service or even the absence from it gives a family identity. From early on, I knew my father had served overseas in the Army Air Force in WWII, and his brother had served in the U.S. Navy during that same war. Service to one's country demands our attention. What happened during those times shaped not only countries. It also restructured families too. Just ask anyone who lost a husband or son or daughter while serving in the military.

LET'S TALK

1. Have you or a family member served in the military during wartime? If so. . .
2. What branch of the service?
3. Which war?
4. What rank was obtained?
5. Where was the term of duty served?
6. What record of the military service do you have?
7. Which medals were received?
8. Discuss family attitudes about service in the military.
9. Were any in your family a "conscientious objector" or "draft protestor?" What happened as a result?

LET'S DISCOVER

1. What different military jobs did you or members of your family hold?
2. If family members were decorated for military heroism, what honors were received?
3. What military tragedies or hardships have affected your family? How were they handled? Consider those who served in Vietnam.

LET'S PLAN

1. Plan to visit a favorite military school, especially if a family member once attended that place. Although none of my family attended West Point located on the Hudson River in New York State, twice we have enjoyed a tour at this beautiful military academy. A visit to the chapel alone makes the trip worthwhile. Even better are the views of the Hudson River from this enviable site along its banks. Plan a trip to the Naval Academy in Annapolis, Maryland, the Air Force Academy in Colorado Springs, Colorado, or the Coast Guard School in New London, Connecticut. All have tours available for visitors.

2. Discover other ways family members have connected themselves to the military. (Consider ROTC, National Guard, or Air National Guard).

3. Did family members serve in a foreign military? Discuss that involvement.

4. Plan to visit national war memorials, such as: Battlefields of the Civil War, Memorials in Washington, DC (Korean War Memorial, Vietnam Memorial, Arlington Cemetery, or the Iwo Jimo Memorial), or Pearl Harbor in Hawaii

5. Attend a military program or event. Consider a Blue Angels Flight Demonstration, a Memorial Day or 4th of July parade, or other military programs or parades sponsored by organizations such as the American Legion or the Veterans of Foreign Wars.

6. Visit or revisit places where either you or family members were stationed. I have often wanted to visit the Island of Vis off the coast of Yugoslavia where my father spent eleven months during World War II repairing bombers.

7. If you were in the military, write or get in touch with other comrades. Plan a reunion, or make arrangements to attend one that someone else has planned. Many military groups held 50th anniversaries of World War II.

8. Preserve the military history of your family. Display medals and uniforms or letters and other papers. I collected and edited 121 letters

my father wrote during World War II and self-published them for family. I have heard of people who collected military patches and even made a quilt from them.

From the days of Ancient Rome, a military draft forced compulsory service. The most unpopular draft in the United States was during Vietnam. Protestors, draft dodgers, and conscientious objectors gave this war a different publicity than any other. I remember those Vietnam War times. No college student could have escaped those troubling years that set a nation on edge.

NINE
SOUL STIRRINGS

Identifying causes that matter to you and your family

Whether literacy ranks as your passion or a Habitat for Humanity project, we all have charitable causes that stir our soul. Maybe you enjoy selling candy bars to help high school band students perform overseas on a good-will tour, or planting flowers in a city party just to make it beautiful.

Causes shape our lives. One of mine was working with mediation. I recall how I had founded a charitable organization that mediated conflicts in both families and in churches, and every mediator volunteered time without a fee. My interest in the field of mediation had a history. As a lawyer, I had found the competitive nature of law especially counterproductive. My growing discomfort caused me to look to new ways to solve problems. The courtroom trial seemed to foster division rather than unity. Mediation, in contrast, was designed to bring about agreement rather than disagreement. I was blessed to see an organization help hundreds make order out of chaos, and find peace where there was only strife.

I wasn't the only one in my family with passions. My father, who served as chairman of the local school board, was opposed to federal aid for education. He believed local school districts would lose control if federal money was accepted. That issue stirred his soul, and he wrote articles for the local paper in support of his opinions.

Discover what matters to you, and you will find what stirs your soul to action.

LET'S TALK

1. What causes did your parents support?
2. What causes do you support? For example, my teenage son thinks all restaurants should ban smoking, a cause unheard of a decade ago.
3. What strong causes have you been involved in? Possibly you participated in the Peace Corps or staged a Vietnam War protest.
4. What causes did your grandparents support? Maybe your ancestors were part of a suffrage movement or participated in a labor strike.
5. Has anyone in your family been involved in a humanitarian effort? What kind?
6. Has anyone in your family been involved in a protest? What method did the protest take – a picket line, a letter writing campaign, or a rally? Did you or someone you know participate in a march?
7. What quiet causes have you or family members supported? Think about delivering meals to the elderly, working at a food shelf, or helping on flood relief.

LET'S DISCOVER

1. Look through a family album. Possibly there will be pictures of family members engaged in charitable work? What organizations are represented? Boy Scouts or Girl Scouts?
2. What causes did you support in the past that you have come to regret? Why was it important at the time? Have you had to mend fences as a result?
3. What causes do young people support today that weren't thought of ten or twenty years ago? Think about environmental issues such as global warming.

4. What life-threatening causes have family members belonged to? How did that affect the family? Did it cause embarrassment? My husband's father was part of the first labor strike in the Minneapolis-St. Paul area. Many of those protestors put their lives on the line

5. What has kept you or family members from joining unpopular causes? Think about family pressure.

LET'S PLAN

1. List five causes that are important to you. How might you become involved in supporting them?

2. Think about giving time or money. If you have received an inheritance, promote causes that were important to your parents. For example, send a child to a camp in honor of a parent

3. What causes do you support? How can you begin if you haven't done so already?

4. If you are over booked with charitable causes, how might you limit your passions?

What particular cause lights up your face? Shakespeare once said, *"Strong reasons make strong actions."* Life without a mission or a cause can become purposeless and shallow. Strong reasons send missionaries across the globe, or prompt the wealthy to give to educational institutions, or stir millions to give to families who lost loved ones in the World Trade Center in New York. Strong reasons can also create misery, especially if they send kids with guns into schools or destroy the property and lives of others. Let your strong reasons be good ones that make this global community in which we live better because you were here.

TEN

THE TABOO OF POLITICS

Learning about political leanings

I was warned: "Don't talk about religion and politics." I grew up thinking everyone was "hatched" from speaking about such matters in public. However, like the kid who grabs at the cookies when told not to, I jumped at every opportunity to discuss those taboo subjects. And I found others willing to talk too.

A high school teacher was more than happy to strike up a lively conversation with me. A portly fellow, Arlen Stangeland would rock back and forth as the two of us would argue political points of view. I would argue that America was becoming too socialized, and he would argue the exact opposite. He, a staunch Democrat, and I, a died-in-the-wool Republican, wouldn't budge on our political views.

And then I met the man I would marry. If political opposites could attract, that would be the two of us. He was an active Democrat, and I was equally committed to the Republican Party. My father questioned whether a marriage based on two political parties could long endure. Fortunately the marriage has lasted nearly thirty years, even though we cancel each other out at the polls.

President Eisenhower described politics as a serious and complicated profession, and Charles de Gaulle said it was too serious to be left to politicians. President John F. Kennedy expressed an entirely different viewpoint: *"The political world is stimulating and the most interesting thing you can do."*

What political persuasions have influenced your life? Think about them.

LET'S TALK

1. What party, if any, has influenced your political viewpoints? Why? Are family members predominately of that party?
2. Recall when you were first introduced to a political party. Was it when you were a child?
3. Have you ever attended a convention or precinct caucus? What role did you have? Have you been a delegate?
4. Have you or family members held public office? Did they run on a political party ticket? What was the campaign like? Did you make phone calls or hand out campaign flyers? Describe that experience.
5. If your family of origin supported a certain political party, what were the reasons for their loyalty? Have you followed that party or changed?
6. Have you or someone in your family run in a non-party election such as a school board or city government position?
7. Was there someone in your family who influenced your political choices? Who?
8. Have you supported a third party candidate such as a Ross Perot or George Wallace or Ralph Nader?
9. Were there negative reactions to "politics" in your family? Did family members think politicians were not to be trusted?

LET'S DISCOVER

1. Do you have old campaign buttons, literature or bumper stickers from by-gone years? Show them to a young person. I wore a Nixon-Lodge button in the 1960 Presidential race even though I was only eleven.
2. Recall how you found out about election winners. My father allowed us

to stay up until 1:00 am on election nights to listen to presidential election returns on the radio, even though we usually didn't know the winner until the following morning. Accustomed to knowing who our next President will be early on election night, the Bush Gore Presidential election frustrated us all. Waiting an unprecedented length of time to know the final results seemed so anti-technology.

3. Where did your parents vote? Did you ever go with them to the polls? My husband and I have taken our young son with us to the polls.
4. Do you vote in all elections? Some? Occasionally?
5. What political issues are important to you? Have you spoken with an elected official about those?

LET'S PLAN

1. Read campaign brochures placed on your door. Actually surprise a candidate and ask them to tell you about their views. They might enjoy the exchange of ideas.
2. Visit your elected officials, whether in your city, state capitol, or Washington, DC. Take an interest in their work.
3. Campaign for someone running for office. You might enjoy distributing literature or walking in a parade.
4. Run for public office yourself. You may want to serve first on a city commission or other public board. Often interested people are selected to fill such appointments.
5. If you were to write a letter to an elected official, what might you say? Write it and then mail it.

The year was 1956, and I was in first grade. I came to school wearing an Eisenhower-Nixon campaign button. Expecting others in the class to agree, I quickly realized other kids in the class didn't have the same political opinions. Others were in favor of someone named Adlai Stevenson. Since that initial experience, I grew up quickly in the world of politics. It was my first lesson in tolerance, and since that time, I've worked for both

Republicans and Democrats in state legislatures and in Washington, DC. I've also learned that there is no need for politicians to dislike each other. I often recall my father, who served in the North Dakota legislature saying that he believed the best legislation was more likely to come out of an evenly divided assembly than one heavily controlled by one party.

One of Minnesota's favorite sons, Vice-President Hubert Humphrey, described politics in these words: *"And here we are, just as we ought to be, here we are, the people, here we are in a spirit of dedication, here we are the way politics ought to be in America, the politics of happiness, the politics of purpose and the politics of joy."* New York Times, April 27, 1968 from a speech delivered in Washington, DC on April 26, 1968.

Wouldn't it be great if more people felt that way? Vote next election. Your vote does make a difference.

ELEVEN
A HOOLA HOOP AND A GAME BOY

Playing around with leisure activities

What do a hoola hoop and a Game Boy have in common? Maybe not much. One requires physical energy and the other operates on battery power. One is best performed outdoors or in a space where there is room to spin, and the other requires minimal space for a kid to zone out on a tiny screen. One is quiet, and the other beeps, squeals and groans.

A hoola hoop and a Game Boy do hold one thing in common – both are entertainment. I purchased a hoola hoop while vacationing in California in 1958 and became one of the first in North Dakota to own this "hot" equipment. Yet, kids today conclude all too readily that something must be missing from their Christmas list if they didn't receive a battery-powered toy.

Entertainment, whether you go to the movies or attend a block party for the neighborhood or call in friends to sing songs around the piano or watch a video together, Americans spend many hours and dollars in pursuit of leisure activities. You may enjoy seeing your child's soccer game or going with friends to a pro baseball game or the football play-offs. It's all

47

entertainment. Your idea of past time may be as simple as playing a board game, making a quilt, or it could be as involved as a trip to Maui to play with the golf pros.

A generation ago, entertainment seemed less complex. Instead of rushing off to the store to purchase more batteries, the dining room table was converted into a ping-pong table, and the kitchen floor, with the table and chairs pushed up against the wall, dubbed as a dance floor for aspiring prom attendees.

Recently I was bemoaning that no one knows how to make his or her own entertainment anymore. Yet the other night, while on an evening walk, my husband and I came across a pleasant sight, reminiscent of the good old days when we converted the kitchen into a ballroom. A couple had backed their car outside their garage, plugged in their compact disc player, and were dancing rock-in-roll in their garage. With no onlookers, this pair appeared to be having the time of their life on their converted dance floor. Maybe we could all take a cue from them and figure out some of our own homemade fun.

LET'S TALK

1. What organized sports did you take part in as a child? Swimming lessons or little league baseball. What organized sports are you or your child involved in today?

2. What athletic opportunities exist today that were not available to you when you were young? Consider women's sports for instance.

3. How did you entertain yourself as a child? Recall such activities as card playing, reading books, board games, playing a musical instrument, sewing, or tinkering with an old car.

4. In what competitive sports or games have you or family members participated? What were or are your feelings about competitive games? What sports do you dislike the most?

5. What outdoor sports or games did you enjoy as a child? Remember hide-and-seek?

Family Archaeology

LET'S DISCOVER

1. Were there games or leisure time activities that were not allowed in your home because of gender or religion or because you didn't have the money? What was your reaction to those restrictions?.

2. How much time do you spend on battery or electronic entertainment such as computer games, television, or Nintendo? A friend of mine has a "battery free" day care center in which original creativity is encouraged. What substitutes can you make for battery-run games?

3. Interview someone from an older generation and ask what types of entertainment they had as a child. Find out what made that entertainment enjoyable.

4. Find out if those from another generation enjoyed particular success as a type of sport or game. Possibly one was an outstanding poker player or always won at Monopoly or fared well at square dancing.

5. What entertainment in the car have you enjoyed while taking long road trips? Anyone in your family enjoy singing?

LET'S PLAN

1. What entertainment do you especially like? (Videos, concerts, games, plays). Do you enjoy spectator sports more than participatory ones? Plan now how you might be involved in one of those activities in the next month.

2. From this list, rank your favorites: _____ read a book, _____ music _____ sports or health club activities, _____ family game activities (board games, cards, or other activities), _____ children's activities (attending their games).

3. What would you like to do next year just for fun?

In the late 1960's, Congress passed laws prohibiting the sale of unsafe toys. Toys with loose, small, or sharp parts or pointed edges were found to be unsafe for children, especially those under three. The Child Protection and Toy Safety Act gave government authority to pull such toys from the market.

I recently attended a one-year-old's birthday party. In the midst of hundreds of dollars of toys, books, and clothes, the child stuck a green bow on the top of her head and smiled from ear to ear. That seemed to be the best present of all.

Children have long loved basic toys like dolls and trucks. They have also loved sand boxes, swimming in rivers and streams, and sledding down a snow-covered hill. Whether a ball, a tricycle, marbles, or a rattle, all of these toys have amused and entertained children for centuries. Then who made toys so complex? Adults or kids? Next time you think about a child's toy, think simple.

TWELVE
A FRIEND IS A FRIEND FOREVER

Identifying friends who made a difference

A childhood friend called, and we arranged a time to get together. Although we hadn't seen each other in years, we giggled like young schoolgirls, and acted more like thirteen-year-olds, than women in our forties. My friend grew-up on the farm next to ours, and even though she was four years younger than I, age didn't separate us. We two buried pet cats killed by passing cars, decorated their graves with flowers stolen from our mother's gardens, and preached sermons for those fallen animals unmatched by our ministers. Friends, especially old friends, endure for a long, long time.

At my husband's high school class reunion, what he enjoyed most was hanging out with his first grade friends. There is something about those old, very old friendships that shape our lives forever.

LET'S TALK

1. Who are some of your old friends? What did you have in common?
2. What makes a friend a friend?
3. Who were some of your mother's friends? What did she like to do with them?

4. Who were some of your father's friends? What interests did they hold in common? Was it a game of poker or going fishing, per chance?
5. What as a child did you enjoy doing with your friends?
6. What do you enjoy doing with friends today?
7. What have you done with a friend this past week?
8. How have friends influenced you for good? Recall a friend who influenced you for bad.

LET'S DISCOVER

1. Find a school yearbook. If friends signed the book, what did they say?
2. If you have an autograph book, look through it. What did friends write in that book?
3. Locate pictures of your parents or grandparents with friends? Were they neighbors? Did they go to the same church, or work in the same jobs, or have similar organizational interests?
4. What friends over the years became like family? Consider how a foreign exchange student became a part of your family.
5. Who did you want as a childhood friend, but it didn't work out?

LET'S PLAN

1. Send a letter or card to a couple old-time friends. Remember them on their birthday, or include them on your Christmas card list.
2. Make a telephone call to an old friend and if they live close by, invite them over for an evening, or plan a meeting spot halfway.
3. Place an autograph book in your guest room. Invite over-night guests to write a note.
4. Invite friends over to your home. Consider including friends from different parts of your life. See how well they mix.
5. Challenge yourself to make a new friend this next year.
6. Strike up a friendship with someone younger than you.

Family Archaeology

By chance we get parents and siblings. By choice we make friends. Even Proverbs 18:24 attests to the great value of a friend: *"A true friend sticks closer than one's nearest kin."* Enjoy your friends.

THIRTEEN
A CLEAN BILL OF HEALTH

Examining your medical history

Imagine how powerful the words, "I'm going to give you a clean bill of health," must sound to someone who has struggle with cancer?

When I asked about membership in a health club, a fitness instructor told me, "I took up aerobics because my family has a history of heart disease and my father died when he was in his forties." Her words struck home, especially since my own mother had died from a heart attack only a few weeks before.

When we visit a doctor's office, we are asked to complete a family history of known medical problems. Doctors know that genetics play a significant role in how healthy we are, because often hidden in our genes are the making of a long healthy life or one crippled by disease.

The disease of hemophilia, buried in the family genes of the Russian Romanov family, shaped and influenced many of this royal family's decisions. Rasputin, believed to have healing powers over the Czar's son, could as a result, exercise considerable control over the Czar's wife, Alexandra, and the entire Russian government. Such was to its detriment. What is hidden in your family genes? Let's find out.

LET'S TALK

1. What childhood illnesses have you had? Talk about the treatment. I had measles and mumps at the same time. My mother claims I was a child to be pitied. Covered with measles on the palms of my hands and the soles of my feet, my throat was also swollen and sore.
2. What immunizations did you receive as a child?
3. Which childhood diseases have later been cured? Think about polio and small pox, for example. Consider whether those diseases could reappear (in light of recent terrorist attacks).
4. What illnesses did your parents or grandparents have? Did poor nutrition or communicable disease affect their health?
5. What conditions affected your health? Where did you go to receive medical care as a child or did your doctor make house calls like my country doctor did?
6. Did you need any emergency medical treatment for appendicitis, cuts, or broken bones?
7. What was your family's attitude about seeking medical care? We had to be terribly sick to be treated by a doctor.

LET'S DISCOVER

1. What medical conditions existed in your family and affected how you lived? My brother had difficulty with his feet. I recall one summer when he was quite young, he had corrective surgery, wore casts on his feet, and we all pitched in to help him out.
2. What measures were taken to accommodate someone in your family with a physical disability? My grandmother lived to be almost 93. My aunt, who was a nurse, cared for her and even moved a hospital bed into her home to help accommodate my grandmother.
3. If you and others in your family have been blessed with "good health." To what do you attribute this blessing? Could it be heredity, good food, healthy conditions, or even good medical care?
4. Talk about longevity in your family. Has a relative lived to be over 90?

5. What physical or mental conditions exist in your family? How have they impacted the quality of life? Talk about such disabilities as depression, loss of hearing, loss of vision, loss of mobility, or mental illness.

LET'S PLAN

1. What can you do to make it possible for you to live better? Which of these are important to you?
2. _____ Exercise
3. _____ Weight control
4. _____ Eating fresh fruit and vegetables
5. _____ Regular doctor visits
6. _____ Playing computer games or watching television
7. _____ Quitting smoking
8. _____ Limiting alcohol use
9. _____ Relaxation (listening to good music, reading uplifting literature, or enjoying time with friends).
10. What are you doing right now that makes you healthier?
11. What would you like to do to contribute to your well-being?
12. What changes are you willing to make this next year in order to have a better and healthier life?
13. Do you have a living will? (Consult with an attorney or a health care provider about this document).

"An apple a day keeps the doctor away?" Whether such an axiom is true, I believed it. Healthy lifestyles are more than doctor appointments. It is how we take care of our bodies in between appointments. Besides sometimes hurried doctor appointments don't really get to the heart of the issue. A notice in the waiting room of an English doctor's office affirms that truth. *"To avoid delay, please have all your symptoms ready."*

FOURTEEN
HOW MUCH IS THE ANOLE IN THE WINDOW?

Making sure pets know their rightful place

People love to talk about their pets. Maybe you've even shared your house with an unusual pet, such as a skunk, rat, or an anole. Let me explain how three green anoles named Agate, Amber, and Albert came to share our household. It started out very innocently. Our son needed to observe a reptile for three weeks in order to meet one of the requirements for his Boy Scout reptile study merit badge.

Since I wasn't interested in harboring a python or iguana in our house, I stated my case for a little painted turtle. Unfortunately, my son wasn't interested in a turtle, and I soon learned that they weren't especially healthy to co-exist with anyway. After visiting several pet shops and even a store that specialized in reptiles, I readily concluded that the three green anoles were the least expensive reptile we could purchase. They only cost $3.99 each. Or so I thought.

We left the pet store with the anoles, a cage, wood chips, a reptile carpet, a heat lamp, and three-dozen crickets, their weekly food supply. The bill ran over $60.00. "Ouch," I said as I wrote out the check. Our son diligently studied the reptiles' habits, recorded data, and qualified for his

59

reptile merit badge.

These five-inch long reptiles amazed us. We noticed how they would change colors, sometimes from a speckled brown to a bright green. Chameleon like, they could blend into their environment so perfectly that we couldn't even spot them in their cage and often wondered where they were hiding. They would cling to the side of the glass cage, their tiny feet acting like suction cups. I'll never forget observing the first feeding. Three-dozen crickets were set loose in the cage. I almost lost my supper when I saw one of the anoles eat a live cricket whole – chirp and all.

I also got concerned when I looked in the cage one day and discovered that Albert had lost part of his tail. Thankfully it grew back, but Albert seemed to change. He became more aggressive and greedy. We would sometimes separate him during feeding times to insure that the other two anoles got some of the crickets. Nevertheless, survival of the fittest proved true in that anole cage. One day we discovered one of the weaker anoles had died. Two remain and are outliving their three-year life expectancy.

Those anoles have kept me busy. It started rather innocently as I have said. Our son needed to observe a reptile for three weeks. But since that purchase, we have been releasing smelly crickets weekly into their cage, and watching these hungry reptiles conquer the defenseless insects. It shouldn't surprise me that though our son has an interest in the reptiles, I am the one who makes the weekly run to the pet shop to pick up the supply of crickets. There's something about a pet. It's hard to let go.

Think about the pets you have let into your home and your heart.

LET'S TALK

1. What childhood pets impacted your life? In what way?
2. What name did you give those pets? If you didn't name them, who did?
3. How long did favorite pets live?
4. What care did those pets require, and who gave them the care they needed?
5. What conflicts did your family experience over pets?

Family Archaeology

LET'S DISCOVER

1. What animals did your parents refuse to have? Although we lived on a farm, my father refused to allow us to have a horse. He must have thought it would be expensive.
2. What stories do you like to tell about pets in your family? What bad behavior do you tolerate in your pet?
3. What pet burial rituals have you observed?
4. What veterinary treatment have your pets required? Don't forget the $900.00 bill you paid to remove a pencil eraser your cat swallowed.
5. Did you take your pet to special obedience training classes? Our miniature pinscher hid under the chairs in the class, but we were able to teach her some commands and to rollover.
6. Have you ever entered a pet in a show? If so, how did your animal perform?
7. Did your pets participate in a children's circus? Try to describe the event without smiling?
8. Have you ever "dressed-up" your pet? How did the animal react?
9. What special toys have you purchased for your pet?
10. What is your favorite animal? Cat . . . dog . . . horse?

LET'S PLAN

1. What type of pet best fits your living situation? Certainly a St. Bernard wouldn't be a good choice for a 10th floor apartment dweller.
2. What unusual pet might you like to own? Check out others who have owned a snake or other unusual pet.
3. What names do you like for animals? There are books with suggestions for names for dogs and cats.
4. What pet would you like to own next?
5. How might you decide what pet to have? Or do you consider it a high-risk choice?

Family Archaeology

Is the dog a man's best friend? Many would agree with that assessment, especially an elderly man who introduced himself at a meeting I attended: *"I'm married and have a dog, and when I come home tonight, they will meet and greet me."* Then he hesitated and added, *"At least the dog will."*

Pets return love instinctively, but humans seem to need bumper stickers to remind them to return that love to their pet. *"Have you hugged your pet today?"*

FIFTEEN
DO I HAVE TO EAT THE
LUTEFISK?

Rediscovering ethnic traditions that have shaped your family

On Christmas Eve my father would cook the lutefisk, and then before any Christmas presents were opened, each of us three children would have to eat some of the slimy white fish that slipped around on our plates. I poured hot butter on the fish to disguise its taste and its looks, but to make matters worse, I feared getting a bone caught in my throat and lutefisk had many bones.

I may not have appreciated eating lutefisk on Christmas Eve then, but in retrospect, what I valued is that we had a rich and full Christmas Eve tradition that my father cared enough to pass on to us. Lutefisk also taught me a valuable lesson in life. Sometimes we have to go through something difficult in order to enjoy the good things that come from such times

But times have changed. We three children have grown up and have families of our own. Instead of celebrating on Christmas Eve, we celebrate on Christmas Day, and instead of opening our presents after a traditional lutefisk meal, we eat our Christmas meal after we have unwrapped our gifts. And probably to no one's surprise, after my father's death, lutefisk was no longer on the Christmas menu. Although this white fish was eliminated from Christmas Eve festivities, certainly the memory of my father and how he loved Christmas Eve would never be forgotten.

I'm not a lutefisk fan, but that slippery fish I ate on Christmas Eve gives me a smile each time I think about it. Traditions give us foundations upon which to build. Whether you are Jewish and celebrate Hanukkah (festival of lights) or Christian and celebrate the birth of Jesus, family traditions remind us that we are part of a bigger celebration. Enjoy traditions. Some of them, you may want to stubbornly pass on to the next generation.

Whether they keep them will be their choice.

LET'S TALK

1. What traditions surrounded your family holiday celebrations? Think especially of Thanksgiving, Christmas, Easter, etc.
2. What ethnic traditions were recognized in your childhood home?
3. What traditions fell by the wayside? How did you react to the change?
4. What traditions, if any, did your family regularly observe? Think about whether your family went to church, had a family devotion, offered a prayer before eating, or ate roast beef every Sunday for dinner.
5. What annual traditions did you observe? Did you visit graves and plant flowers on Memorial Day, watch fireworks on the Fourth of July, or go to a lake home on Labor Day weekend?

LET'S DISCOVER

1. Look through a photo album. Do any of the pictures show traditions? We always took a picture at the table before eating our Christmas meal. We would set up the camera for a timed photo, and then the photographer would pop into the picture just as the camera would capture the biggest smiles on our faces.
2. Ask your parents, siblings or other family members if they can recall traditions that were important in your family. You may be surprised what they remember.
3. How did your traditions differ from your neighbors'?

LET'S PLAN

1. What family traditions would you like to continue or even expand?

2. Based on your ethnic, family, community, or religious background, what new traditions would you like to start? My husband's family for a number of years celebrated St. Urho's day on the 16th of March. The legend says that St. Urho drove the grasshoppers out of Finland and save the grape crop. Of course this holiday isn't even known in Finland. It's entirely an American invention.

3. Rethink some family traditions you enjoyed as a child and then reincorporate them into your own celebrations. You may find them rather delightful. I haven't been able to bring myself around to reintroduce lutefisk, however.

4. What traditions do neighbors or other family members have that you would like to adopt?

5. Ask a friend what traditions or rituals his or her family observes. Think how you could introduce some of the good ones into your own family life.

6. Make a scrapbook or picture book of your family engaged in some tradition.

7. How do you resolve traditions from two different family backgrounds? Who wins?

8. How do you plan on passing on traditions when the next generation doesn't appear to be interested?

Henry James said, *"It takes an endless amount of history to make even a little bit of tradition."* Traditions are hard won, yet worth the effort. They can give an inestimable sense of identity and purpose.

SIXTEEN
FAVORITES

Putting a name to things you and your family love

If you had an afternoon entirely to yourself, what would you do? I told a friend I would sit by a pool in a warm place, drink a Diet Coke, and write on my lap top computer. Others might visit an adult child or spend time with a grandchild. Booklovers might want to curl up with a good novel, and others would head for the golf course.

We all have different favorites. My husband loves to read about Civil War Battles, even though I've tried to convince him that war is over. He loves to visit national battlefields, and I've learned, ever so painfully, to appreciate his favorite things as much as he has learned to appreciate mine. Every so often he will sit and listen while I play my piano, a definite favorite of mine.

I've discovered, however, appreciating his favorite things has also expanded my own. Yes, it's good to seek out a few of your favorite things so "you don't feel so bad," but it is also fun to discover what tickles other people's fancies. In doing so, you might find new ones of your own. What are your favorites? Could they be . . ?

"Raindrops on roses, whiskers on kittens, bright copper kettles and warm woolen mittens . . . When I'm feeling said, I simply remember my favorite things and then I don't feel so bad."

Family Archaeology

LET'S TALK

1. What were some of your favorite activities as a child? Who enjoyed them with you?
2. What did your family enjoy doing together? Think about games or travel or camping.
3. What "favorite" people did you visit?
4. What favorite spots did you visit as a child? Would you like to plan a trip back there?
5. Talk about some of your favorite school subjects, activities, and teachers? What made them favorites? Was it the subject matter or the teacher who taught you?
6. What favorite automobile did you own? Was it your first car?
7. Did you have a secret get-away? Think about a place you found especially welcoming. What did you like about that place?
8. Talk about a favorite pet. What happened to the animal?

LET'S DISCOVER

1. What favorite activities do you like to do with others?
2. What are some of your favorite groups? Possibly the group is a musical one or a book club or a children's club such as 4-H or Scouts.
3. Think about the following favorites and rank them according to your interests:
4. _____ Watching sports on television
5. _____ Reading a novel
6. _____ Eating out in restaurants
7. _____ Listening to a musical group or participating in one
8. _____ Going out to a movie
9. _____ Attending a play
10. _____ Doing a sport's activity like running, biking, or aerobics.
11. _____ Travel in the USA
12. _____ Travel outside the USA (name your favorite place)

13. What are your favorite readings? Think of Biblical texts or poetry. What makes them endearing to you? I've always loved Psalm 90 because it was read at my mother's funeral.
14. What are your favorite foods? How often do you eat them?
15. What are your favorite hobbies?

LET'S PLAN

1. What book or series of books would you like to read? Schedule a special reading time each day.
2. What is the favorite part of your present job? What might you enjoy in a future employment? What changes might that require?
3. Where do you like to shop? Do hardware, clothing, or grocery stores attract you? Plan to visit a new store. It might become a favorite.
4. Name five favorite things you would like to do in the next years. It may be a trip to a place you've always wanted to visit. For example, I have always wanted to see the giant sequoia trees in California. Last year that dream came true.
5. Plan how to make dreams come true.
6. Plan a meeting with those you live with. Find out what each person likes to do, and then begin setting aside time and money to make those dreams come true. For example, my son has a dream of having a high-powered telescope. We are working on a plan to make that hope and dream come true.
7. Seek ways to make favorite activities happen more often. It might be lunch with a friend or a visit to a favorite arboretum.

I was struck by the words of Henry Fielding who said, *"Every physician hath his favorite disease."* We all have favorites. What are yours? Take time this week to rediscover what delights you.

SEVENTEEN
AN APPLE FOR THE TEACHER

Praising teachers who went beyond the book

A teacher affects eternity. My piano teacher was one of them. The smell of a fresh shower and fragranced powder filled her living room where she patiently worked me through the red John Thompson piano books. This teacher even taught my brother and me a duet, which we performed at our first piano recital. My brother didn't stick to his piano lessons, but he can still play the opening stanza of *Lieberstraum,* which Mrs. Strand taught him.

I continued piano lessons, but I remember the day when my piano teacher told me she could not take me any further and that I should study under one of the teachers at the high school. Heartbroken, I left her living room that afternoon, knowing that this dear teacher had taught me more than scales. She had taught me about life. Her pleasant demeanor, her fifty-cent lessons, and her commitment to her music students taught me that a teacher often by teaching one subject teaches yet another.

When I would return to my hometown for visits, my piano teacher would always ask: "Are you still playing the piano?" I would reassure her that I played a little each day. Her eyes would twinkle, as a broad smile would sweep across her plump, pleasing face.

I've had many teachers – Sunday school teachers, elementary school

71

teachers, high school, college, and law school teachers. But one stands above the rest – my piano teacher, who taught me about music and life. She affected me forever.

At a Lorie Line concert, the performing artist, who had even performed before White House audiences, was asked whom she would like to perform for. She paused and then said with a smile,, "Although I can't because she died, I would love to play for my piano teacher."

LET'S TALK
1. Which teacher influenced you and in what ways?
2. How would you describe that teacher?
3. Recall your kindergarten or first grade teacher. Describe that teacher to someone.
4. Think about sports, music, or religion teachers you have had. What lasting impressions did they make on you?
5. Think about a teacher you disliked. What was the reason? How did that teacher affect you?

LET'S DISCOVER
1. Think back on favorite teachers. What did you like about them?
2. _____ The discipline they used.
3. _____ How they made you feel important
4. _____ The methods they used to instruct you
5. _____ The subject they taught
6. _____ How they encouraged you to pursue a particular career
7. Use one word to describe a teacher who influenced you in elementary school, high school, college, or in post college education.
8. Consider teachers you have had in your adult years? Do you remember them?
9. Which teacher took a difficult subject and made it easy?

LET'S PLAN

1. Write a teacher and thank that educator for the influence he or she had on your life. Do not put this off before it is too late.
2. Plan a party for a favorite teacher. Gather up memory letters from both current and former students and present them at the party. For example, you could present such a treasure to a piano teacher at the spring music recital.
3. Write a letter to a school and let the administration know about a teacher who has helped either you or a child of yours.
4. If you are a teacher, write a letter to a favorite former student. Let them know what made them a joy to teach.
5. Write a piece about a teacher for a local historical society. Include a picture if possible. Maybe a local paper would appreciate such a remembrance too.
6. Think about teachers in nontraditional settings such as clubs like 4-H, or Boy Scouts or Girl Scouts or even a neighbor who taught you how to shoot a rifle or an older cousin who gave you driving lessons. What made their teaching stick with you?

Ralph Waldo Emerson described an educator as one who makes hard things easy. Recall those teachers in your life who were able to unravel the difficult and make it understandable. Such a teacher is more precious than gold. Don't you agree?

EIGHTEEN
GOOD FENCES MAKE GOOD
NEIGHBORS

―――

Recalling neighbors and how they bordered your life

R obert Frost captured one aspect of being a good neighbor in these words: "'*My apple trees will never get across and eat the cones under his pines,*' I tell him. He only says, '*Good fences make good neighbors.*'" In neighborly relations, minding your own business is important, yet on other occasions when tragedy strikes, the welcome smile of a neighbor can mean more than the distant concern of family who no longer live close.

With the news of my mother's death heavy on my heart, upon my arrival home, it was our neighbors who were first on the scene with food and love.

I'm ashamed to admit this, but I don't know much about my neighbors to the south of me. I don't know how old they are, whether they have children, or even where they work. I wouldn't recognize them because I've never seen them. Between our lot lines, a fence towers so high that neither of us can look over it. What I've discovered is that good fences instead of making good neighbors can make no neighbors.

I must disappointment neighbors who like to maintain meticulous lawns and have endless hours to putter and plant and prune. When I set foot on my lawn, about all I can manage to do is push my foot to the pedal of my riding lawn mower and hope and pray it doesn't rain before the job gets done.

Even if there isn't an actual fence, the invisible fences of fear and distrust also keep us from getting to know our neighbor.

LET'S TALK

1. When you were growing up, who were your neighbors? Describe them.
2. What effect did they have on your family? Did they become like family?
3. What did you share in common? For example, churches or schools or friends. Maybe you shared participation in a civic club or fraternal organization.
4. Who are your neighbors now? What do you know about them? Do you think there are things they may not want you to know?
5. Do you know more about Hollywood stars and political figures than you do about the people who live next door? Why do you think that has occurred?

LET'S DISCOVER

1. What do your neighbors know about you? Are there things you don't want them to know?
2. How long have you had the same neighbors?
3. What makes a person a "good neighbor?"
4. What impression does your neighbor's home and yard leave?

LET'S PLAN

1. Visit a neighborhood in which you use to live. You may want to knock on the door and find out who lives in your old home. Have you ever done this?
2. Send a card or write a note to a neighbor. Recall a happy time you spent with them.
3. Attend a national night out. Make a list with phone numbers of all your neighbors. Keep it updated each year.

4. Think of ways to be a better neighbor.
5. What would you like your neighbors to remember about you?
6. In a global community, how might you be concerned about neighbors who live in another part of the US or the world? Consider reconnecting by e-mail.
7. Pick a neighbor you have never met and say hello.

"In the field of world policy, I would dedicate this nation to the policy of the good neighbor." Franklin Delano Roosevelt said these words in his 1933 Inaugural Address. In 1939, the world would undergo the most devastating war in the history of humankind; a war that would cost the United States nearly a half a million lives.

What does it mean to be a good neighbor?

A young Jewish leader asked Jesus that question. Jesus told him that the good neighbor is the one who extended the hand of friendship to those who are different than we are. In a world accessible with the simple click of a mouse, we have reconfigured the whole concept of a neighborhood. The earth is our community, and that includes Afghanistan.

NINETEEN
FOLLOW THE LEADER

Identifying leaders in your family

Walter Lippman said, *"Leaders are the custodians of a nation's ideals."* He used these words to describe leaders. Family leaders become custodians of family values. Leaders may emerge in families in unusual ways. Location, birth order, natural ability, or even gender may play a part in the selection process. Even a crisis may give cause for a leader to rise who wasn't considered a family leader before. Or the death of one member of the family may signal the passing of the baton to another.

Who are your family leaders? Of what ideals and traditions have they become the custodian?

LET'S TALK

1. Who were the leaders in your grandparents' or parents' homes? Do you know? Ask someone, if you don't know. Don't be surprised if you get different responses.
2. What gave those leaders authority? Consider whether it was gender, self-appointment, location, or their birth order that gave them a position of influence.

3. What are the characteristics of leaders in your family? Which of those traits are attractive? Which are not?

4. Who in your family arranges the get-togethers? Is it usually the same person or does the responsibility become a shared one? Do you like the arrangement?

5. What leadership qualities do you possess? Why or why wouldn't you be considered the leader?

6. Do you find it hard to follow the leader or leaders in your family? Might you be envious of their role?

LET'S DISCOVER

1. Find out about leadership roles in other families. What makes those families click?

2. Who was the leader in your family of origin? Consider whether it was your mother, your father, or a sibling. Possibly an uncle or grandparent remained the leader even though they didn't live in your home. How did they exercise control from a distance?

3. Who is the leader in your family now? Has it changed? If so, when?

4. What attitudes did you grow up with about leadership roles?

5. What fears do you have about holding a leadership position either in your family, at work, or in an organization?

6. What current leadership roles do you have and what is your reaction to them? Talk about a difficult leadership position you held? What did you do as a result? Quit, slug it out, or turn the situation around?

7. Tell another person about a leadership position you held and liked. Don't forget to mention if a teamwork spirit existed. A flight attendant told me "the team atmosphere" is what makes a big difference in how a flight progresses. What leadership qualities do you possess? How have they helped you? Maybe you have an ability to get everyone together for that family photo.

8. Tacitus (55 – 130 AD) said that reason and judgment were the most important traits for a leader to possess. What do you think are the most important characteristics?

Family Archaeology

9. What has been the price you have paid for leadership? Maybe there has been a falling out between you and another family member.

LET'S PLAN

1. What leadership roles might you take in the future in your: Family_____ Work_____ Neighborhood_____ Organizations_____ Church or synagogue_____.
2. What leadership qualities would you like to have?
3. What would you like to take charge of in your family? (Consider launching the next family reunion)
4. If your family has no natural leader, are you willing to do something about it? What have you noticed when a family has no leadership?
5. How can leadership be shared in a family?
6. Donald McGannon said, *"Leadership is action, not position."* What family leadership action would you like to take in the next six months to make your family stronger, work more cooperatively, and be more cohesive? For example, instead of talking about an unmarked grave in the family, one family member collected the money and ordered a footstone to identify the deceased.

Henry Ford, when asked the question, *"Who ought to be the boss?"* gave this response: *"It's like asking who ought to be the tenor in the quartet. Obviously, the one who can sing tenor."*

Leadership roles in families may not be as obvious. In some cases, an oldest child is selected or expected to be leader regardless of desire or ability. Such a one may find, even without being asked, his name on powers-of-attorney or other legal documents. In other instances, family responsibilities may be shared or alternated. Experts in group dynamics have concluded, however, when no leader emerges, a group will find itself unable to accomplish its mission.

Calling all leaders. Step forward.

TWENTY
RICE ARONI
THE SAN FRANCISCO TREAT

Salivating over ethnic food

Falafel, baklava, and lefse. Ethnic foods like these add zest to ordinary fare. A couple of winters ago, my brother announced that he had purchased a lefse grill for Christmas. I took his comment as a hint that it was time for one of the women to learn how to make this Norwegian ethnic food – a flat potato bread that tastes great rolled up with butter and brown sugar. So I was surprised when my brother made this unusual holiday food himself. His desire to do baking brought back fond memories of Christmas time when my father would make several batches of Fattigman, also known as the "Poor Man's Cookie." He would first dip the dough into hot sizzling oil, remove them with tongs, and fold them into triangles. When the baking was completed, my father would sprinkle generous amounts of powdered sugar on them, and set them in a cool place. I grew to love this messy Christmas treat.

My first experience with ethnic cooking came through 4-H, when I decided to demonstrate making lasagna. Back in the early 1960s, this ethnic dish was as foreign to the American home as the pizza. Some of us recall he complexities of making a pizza. It was far more involved than getting layers of wrappings ripped off a frozen pizza and popping it in the oven for eighteen minutes. First we had to let the dough rise for the crust, and then attempt to stretch it to the edges of a cookie sheet without leaving gapping holes. After making a few patches to the dough, tomato sauce and cheese were sprinkled on top. These first attempts at making pizza were nothing to brag about. Yet, in spite of all its problems, Americans love for pizza has not dwindled in the past forty years. In fact, this Americanized Italian dish has successfully woven its way into the hearts of the American people. So much, that I expect someday kids in America will think pizza is an American dish.

LET'S TALK

1. When were you first introduced to the foods of another culture? What was your reaction and who were you with?
2. Did you grow up with foods of a particular ethnic group? If so, what were they?
3. Who cooked ethnic foods in your family? Were special recipes passed on to another generation? Would you share a 'secret' family recipe with others?
4. What ethnic foods do you still enjoy, simply because you acquired a taste for them as a child? Several of my Norwegian relatives just can't seem to resist lutefisk (white cod fish) and even enjoy going to church festivals that serve this slimy dish. They must be part of a movement that enjoys bumper stickers that say, "legalize lutefisk."
5. What ethnic foods have you come to enjoy as an adult? Who introduced them to you? I recall eating my first falafel in Israel and now I enjoy going to a Middle Eastern café that makes them.
6. What do you do when you are served an ethnic food you don't like? Princess Diana once said, "You wouldn't believe what I have eaten for the sake of England."

LET'S DISCOVER

1. What family recipes do you have for ethnic foods?
2. Would you like some easy-to-follow directions for what otherwise may be rather complex food dishes? Where might you go to get such help?

3. What methods of cooking did your parents or grandparents use to make certain ethnic foods?
4. Find out the origin of dishes in your family? For example, did your family make a certain dish because the garden produced an abundance of potatoes, squash, or turnips?
5. What special preparations were necessary to make certain foods? I'm told that Lutefisk is cured in lye prior to cooking.
6. What national or ethnic dishes are most popular in your family? Mexican anyone?
7. What ethnic fast-food places have made a hit with your family – such as a Taco John's or Pizza Hut or a Chinese Kitchen?
8. Discover why certain foods are so strongly identified with a certain country? For example rice is ethnically connected to Asian countries because so much of it grows there.
9. Describe eating experiences you have had while traveling outside the U.S.A?
10. What ethnic food did you leave on the plate? (The eye of the fish, for example?)

LET'S PLAN

1. What are some of your favorite ethnic foods? Don't forget about egg rolls.
2. Start an ethnic foods group. Bring different ethnic foods to parties until someone gets brave enough to do the whole meal or hires a French chef to do it for you.
3. Learn the history of certain foods. You may enjoy knowing that the Earl of Sandwich named the two slices of bread with roast beef in the center a "sandwich." The name stuck, and expanded to include almost any and every kind of food served on bread.
4. Visit three or four new ethnic restaurants each year. Take notes on your experience and ask plenty of questions how the food was prepared. If you live in a metropolitan area you are more likely to find taste

opportunities such as these. However, even if you come from any area where the only restaurant in town serves hamburgers, you can incorporate a foreign restaurant experience into your annual vacation.

5. If your area is large enough, start a restaurant group that visits several different ethnic restaurants each year. You may also be fortunate enough to find a dining facility that offers live music from that culture.

6. Put together an ethnic cookbook. Ask family members to contribute their favorite recipes and sell the cookbooks at cost (or a profit if you dare) at the next family reunion.

7. Order take-out this week. Try Chinese or Tai.
    Make plans to attend a festival of nations. Make sure you are very hungry, and then sample unusual foods without paying the cost of a sit down dinner. Note which foods you especially liked and then try to make some of them at home. You can find recipes often times on the Internet.

8. Collect ethnic cookbooks and resolve to try one new recipe a month. Make sure the dog doesn't gain weight.

9. Go to an ethnic grocery store. Find out what's available for purchase.

10. Have someone do an ethnic food demonstration. You may be surprised how much you can learn.

Did you know that monks in Southern Europe made the first pretzels and gave them out as rewards for students who learned their prayers? The crossed ends represented praying hands. Pretzels aren't the only food with a story behind it. Possibly your own family has created a dish or two and the recipe and a story has been passed down to another generation. Enjoy both!

TWENTY-ONE
KNIT TWO, PURL TWO

Prospering what you do with your hands and other handcraft skills in your family

My Norwegian grandmother knew how to knit and she did it well. I am told, after the supper meal when the children were in bed, she would knit. She knit out of necessity, but no doubt she enjoyed this art too. Each Christmas each of the nine children would receive a new pair of mittens and cap. Even today Norwegians are known for their knitting ability, and primary schools in Norway require all students (yes, even the boys) to learn this skill.

Your family will have different handicraft skills. Those abilities may have contributed to the livelihood of a family (my husband's grandfather was a shoemaker), or benefitted the family in some direct way (sewing clothing, for example), or were purely for pleasure (women quilt for fun). Whatever the case, you may want to take up a new craft or return to an old one and rediscover the pleasures that can come from doing something with your hands.

Family Archaeology

LET'S TALK

1. What handicraft skills did you enjoy as a child? Maybe you liked to embroider or bake cookies.
2. What particular handicraft skills did your parents have? My mother enjoyed crocheting and loved to make afghans. My father enjoyed working with wood and refinished an old piano for me.
3. What hand-skills do members of your family possess? Do you have a brother who can fix anything and a husband who considers changing a light bulb working with electricity?
4. What particular handicraft skills have won prizes? Think about county or state fairs. Did you get a white ribbon or did your chest puff up a little when you won that purple sweepstakes ribbon?
5. What particular handicraft talents do you have? What particular handicraft talents would you like to have? Think about sewing, baking, or home decorating.
6. Who encouraged you to develop certain hand-skills?

LET'S DISCOVER

1. What handicraft talents are displayed in your home? Think about wreaths you have made, photos you have taken, curtains you have sewed, or a piece of furniture you have refinished.
2. What crafts have your children done? Did you teach them or did they learn from someone else? Where are these talents displayed? On your refrigerator? An older man who took up painting was asked what he was going to do with his "Rembrandts?" He informed his inquirers that he was going to send them to his children so they could put them on their refrigerators.
3. What crafts have you enjoyed in the past?
4. What keeps you from those crafts now? _____ Lost interest_____ No time_____ No longer the thing to do _____ Lack of money_____ Went on to bigger and better things

5. What handicraft was popular for a time and then interest in it faded? For example, I don't see many people making macramé rope flowerpot hangers anymore.
6. What gifts have you made for others? What was their reaction? Did they really like the gift or simply say, "thank you" to be polite?
7. What have you learned to do because your child was learning the craft? My mother took up knitting when I enrolled in a 4-H knitting class.
8. What children's projects became more adult centered than originally intended? Think about those pinewood derby cars you made when your son was in Cub Scouts.
9. What benefits did you receive from doing a craft?

LET'S PLAN

1. What craft would you like to pursue in the next year?
2. What education or class might help? What books will you need?
3. Which of the following interests you?

____ furniture refinishing
____ painting birdhouses or dollhouses
____ water color
____ calligraphy
____ card making
____ knitting or crocheting
____ ethnic stitchery such has Hardanger
____ string art
____ weaving
____ quilting
____ woodworking
____ flower pressing
____ ceramics
____ sculpting
____ photography
____ rubber stamping
____ memory scrapbooks

_____ stenciling

_____ flower arranging

_____ cross-stitch

_____ working with dolls

_____ leatherwork

_____ baking

_____ cooking

_____ jewelry making

_____ sewing

_____ creating period costumes (try creating Civil War and Victorian costumes)

_____ book binding

_____ stain glass works

4. I have always wanted to make _____. I would like to find out if I have an interest in _____. I respect _____ ability to _____. I would like to give _____ my_____

5. Check out class offerings at your local craft store, fabric store, or community education offerings.

You can find enjoyment making grandfather clocks, calligraphy greeting cards, or maybe you would like to crochet a baby blanket, or try a new craft. So find out what whets your fancy and then whittle away the hours.

TWENTY-TWO
COUNT TO TEN IN LATIN

Learning linguistics

Did you know there are over 6000 languages in the world? As a child I enjoyed learning how to count to ten in different languages. My mother, who had studied Latin, taught me how to count to ten in what she considered a "dead" language. My father, who spoke Norwegian until he entered first grade, taught me how to speak to ten in Norse. en, to, tre, fire, fem, seks, sju . . .

Language is more than counting to ten, but the words we use and their sounds communicate who and what we are. Through language we express ourselves. One painful example comes to mind. I recall visiting my Norwegian relatives in Molde, Norway when I was in my early 30s. Since I did not know more than a "thank you" and a "hello", the afternoon grew very long without an interpreter available to help us make sense of our deepest yearnings. It is out of the need to express our wants and desires that languages are born.

There is another language of the human soul. Carl Sandburg, poet laureate from Illinois expressed it in this question: "When shall we all speak the same language?" He wasn't campaigning for a universal language, as those who introduced Esperanto intended. He was advocating an understanding that transcends words. Yet, knowing another language helps us do exactly that.

Family Archaeology

LET'S TALK

1. What languages were spoken in your home or in the home of grandparents or great grandparents? Did you learn that language? If so, who taught you?
2. How many languages can you understand or speak?
3. When you travel in foreign countries do you depend on others knowing English?
4. Talk about your experience speaking a foreign language while visiting that country?
5. Do you have some embarrassing moments speaking a foreign language?
6. When were you last impressed with others ability to converse in several different languages? I will never forget a businessman we met on board a train from St. Petersburg, Russia to Helsinki, Finland. This diplomat spoke flawless English, even though he had never been in the United States, and that's not all. He knew six other languages fluently too.
7. What training have you had in foreign languages? How did you benefit from that education?
8. What songs in a foreign language can you sing?

LET'S DISCOVER

1. What languages do you consider superior? For example, years ago the wealthy nobility in the German courts spoke the French language which was considered a more eloquent language. The kitchen help spoke the common, guttural German.
2. What languages fascinate you and why?
3. What letters, church records, or legal documents do you have that are written in a foreign language? Have those papers been translated?
4. What books written in a foreign language have been passed down to you? Consider hymnals and prayer books that ancestors may have owned.
5. Have you or other members of your family been in a position where you needed to learn a foreign language? A nephew joined the Peace Corps

and spent the first several weeks in a French immersion language course in Paris before going to Abidjan, Ivory Coast.

6.   When in a foreign country have you found an interpreter essential? We would not have been able to communicate with our Russian driver were it not for an interpreter who spoke both English and Russian.

7.   What special efforts have you or family members made to learn a foreign language? The story is told that my Norwegian grandfather taught himself English. He took his language books and studied in the woodshed. Now that is self-taught.

LET'S PLAN

1.   What language might you be interested in studying? Where could you take a course or would you rather buy tapes at a bookstore and study on your own? Set up some goals. Learn how to say thank you or write a simple letter.

2.   Listen to other languages for the sounds and beauty – even if you don't understand the words. Everyone can learn to appreciate an Italian opera.

3.   Think about words that have been added to your language each year. You may want to purchase an updated dictionary to keep up-to-date.

4.   Learn a song in a foreign language.

5.   Visit a foreign country this next year and see how much you can communicate in that language. Start with a menu in a restaurant.

6.   Talk to a Bible translator. Find out how they learn the language of a tribe, and then reduce it to writing. Ask how long such a project can take. You may be surprised to learn that it can take a lifetime.

7.   Learn the sign language alphabet.

8.   Have you ever made up a secret language that was all your own? Rather than go outdoors for recess, several of us girls in grade school stayed inside and made up our own secret language. We swore to never let anyone in on the code. Words like "love" were carefully coded into this secret fifth grade language. We could let others know we were infatuated over a certain boy and the others in the class (especially the boys) would never know.

TWENTY-THREE
SHE LOOKS LIKE, SHE ACTS
LIKE, SHE IS LIKE

Exploring similarities and differences and why some married couples look alike

I held the one-week infant in my arms searching for something to say. Finally, I blurted out: "She looks just like you." The mother grinned, pleased that her child bore some similarity to her. On other occasions, people lack words to say when looking at a newborn. Possibly you have said something as ridiculous as, "Now there's a baby."

There are no bad looking families. All look good when photographed together. The unique blend of characteristics of parents and children always make for wonderful pictures.

Family comparisons fascinate us, whether we compare facial features or mannerisms or even speech patterns. Families make interesting studies, and not just for geneticists. We're all curious about our ancestors. Van Wack Brooks understood that curiosity when he wrote, *"Nothing is so soothing to our self-esteem as to find our bad traits in our forbearers. It seems to absolve us."*

Family Archaeology

LET'S TALK

1. What physical traits of your parents do you possess? Consider height, size, hair coloring, facial features, shoe size, and even how you talk.
2. What similar career interests do family members have? For example almost everyone in my husband's family has a love for rocks, even those without the degree in geology.
3. How do you physically differ from your parents or siblings?
4. What nervous habits appear in your family and have been passed on to the next generation? Is your family full of nail biters or hair twisters?
5. What negative traits exist in your family? Does a cousin of yours have the worse cackle imaginable, and do addictions and that bad temper keep reappearing in successive generation?
6. What negative traits did you inherit?
7. What positive attributes have been passed on through generations? Possibly your family has a philanthropic bent and has taken in foster children or refugees over the years.

LET'S DISCOVER

1. What professions or careers have family members pursued that are similar? For example in my family many became school teachers or continued a tradition of farming.
2. Take a look at family photographs. What is similar? What differences do you notice?
3. Ask someone in your family who you are most like?
4. Notice voice tonal qualities among family members. Recall a time when someone on the phone thought you were someone else in the family. My husband once called his brother's home. His wife mistook him for her husband and before he could barely say hello, she blurted out, "Remember to bring home some bread."
5. What disabilities exist in your family? What encouragement can you provide for others with these limitations?

6. What similar traits have adopted children picked up from your family's home environment?

LET'S PLAN

1. Study pictures of ancestors. Enjoy the comparison.
2. Put together a family cookbook. Ask everyone to bring favorite recipes. Find out who has similar taste buds. Did more recipes for desserts appear or more for meat and potatoes?
3. Celebrate similar achievements in your family with a *"like father – like son"* or *"like mother – like daughter."* My brother even holds some of the same offices in various organizations that my father held. Two of my first cousins won the same "Outstanding Homemaker in South Dakota" award that our great grandmother had won several generations before. History repeats itself.
4. I believe I am most like _____ in my family.

Oliver Wendell Holmes described heredity as *"an omnibus in which all our ancestors ride, and every now and then one of them puts his head out and embarrasses us."*

Relatives may bear similar habits, even though they have never seen each other. My mother-in-law visited her Finnish relatives only to discover that some of them had the same speech patterns relatives had in the USA. They had never met.

If you understand your roots, you may be able to understand yourself. Woodrow Wilson said, *"Ones rootage is more important than his leafage."* Do you agree?

TWENTY-FOUR
MOTHERHOOD AND APPLE PIE

Reclaiming family traditions and values that endure

Thomas Paine said, *"What we obtain too cheaply, we esteem too lightly; it is dearness only that gives everything its value."* What do you value? What's important to you?

A person's checkbook and appointment calendar disclose two very important value systems – where we spend our money, and how we use our time.

Before I had a child, I gave little thought to the value of motherhood, but now that I have a son, I would be offended if Mother's Day slipped by without a mention.

Maybe apple pie isn't a favorite, unless, of course, you are struggling to find a buyer for your home and are told that the smell of an apple pie baking in your oven just might seal the deal. Circumstances change what we value. Frequent flyer miles are no longer of value to a person who has lost his health, and for one, who has inherited large sums of money; the value of hard work may have diminished appeal.

What do you value? Think it over. Is it motherhood, apple pie, and the American flag? Is it the United States of America and the religious freedom we have here? What helps you make decisions? Is it your religious convictions or the values your parents taught you? For now, roll back time a generation or two and consider what your parents or grandparents valued.

Family Archaeology

Possibly their choices not only affected them lives, but generations to come. Certainly my grandfather, who emigrated from the fjords of Norway to farm the flat prairies of North Dakota, could not have known that decision would affect generations after him who still carry on a farming tradition there. Nor could my great grandfather, who ranched near Spearfish, South Dakota, have known his decision would affect three later generations who continue a tradition of cattle ranching.

LET'S TALK

1. Think about the last big expenditure you made. Was it a trip to Hawaii or did you pay for college tuition for your child or did you purchase new living room furniture or did you fund a humanitarian trip to build homes for a poor family? What does that expenditure reveal about your values?

2. What did your parents value? Possibly it was family get-togethers or carrying on a family business or simply hard work. Maybe getting a good education was important. My husband's parents regretted only having eighth grade educations and as a result, encouraged all of their children to get college degrees – and they all did.

3. What values did your parents impress upon you? Was it early to bed, early to rise?

4. What importance was placed on owning possessions or land? How has that impacted how you live?

5. What religious values are important in your family? Think about attending church, reading the Bible, or helping out the poor.

LET'S DISCOVER

1. Look through old family albums. What family values do those picture reveal? Look for that proud teenager in front of his first car or sporting his letterman's jacket.

2. What importance did your parents or other family members place on education?

3. What values did your family question? What was the result?

4. What attitudes did your family have about work? What impact have those had on your career choices?
5. What value was placed on family gatherings? Haven't you noticed how some families just seem to like to get together regardless of the reason?
6. What personal possessions have value in your family? Think about the rock collection, or the stamp collection or the photo albums.
7. How have your values changed over your lifetime? What do you value now that you didn't consider important a decade ago? I once asked a group of college freshman what they thought was most important and they answered, "weekends." I asked an unhappy married woman what was most difficult for her and she said, "weekends." It's all perspective.

LET'S PLAN

1. Ask family members what they value. A businessman said it's important to him to arrive home by 6:00 in the evening so he could eat the evening meal with his wife and family – even if that meant returning to the office later that evening.
2. What clashes with your values? What changes will you make?
3. List what you consider important. Ask your spouse or children to tell you what they consider important. Talk about differences.
4. Rethink the list you pulled together. Ask which of those will have value a hundred years from now.
5. How can you let a younger person know what you value? A while ago I decided to purchase savings bonds or a collection of coins minted in the year of the child's birth for baby gifts, rather than give clothing.
6. Think back on happy moments. What made them important?
7. Write about cherished moments in a special notebook. You may want to add some pictures as well to the memoir. When you are feeling discouraged, read about these special times. It will cheer your day.

Booth Tarkington said, *"The cherished moments we collect each day make a fine cushion for old age."* Gather abundantly!

TWENTY-FIVE
PLANNING A FAMILY REUNION

Looking for kindred spirits

Why would you want to attend a family reunion? Think about it. Possibly a cousin from Sweden is visiting in America and the reunion has been scheduled at the same time. Maybe it is the centennial of your great grandfather's birthday, and you would like to reconnect with some of your kin. Maybe you have been away from family for decades and would like to know more about them.

Whatever your reasons for coming to a family reunion, meeting your fourth cousin once removed, won't cut it. You will need strong reasons for showing up. Then again, why not just say, "We are family." That is a sufficient enough reason.

Maybe you were asked to be on the committee to plan a family reunion. Did you say "yes" before you had time to think about it, and now family pride gives you no avenue of escape? Don't despair. The following ideas will help you create a successful and memorable occasion, but remember plan, plan, plan.

THE LEAD TIME

Allow sufficient lead time. A family reunion takes time to plan, and unless your family hosts an event like this once each year at the same place and time, you will need ample time to pull the gathering together. Give yourself one or two years to find names and addresses, make facility arrangements, and find needed reunion help. You may need more time if you are compiling a family history book. Such efforts could take more than three years.

CREATING INTEREST

Create excitement for the event. Family reunions might sound boring at first blush. Families need to be drawn to the event, especially if they will be coming hundreds of miles. Here are a few ways you can generate excitement:

1. Create interest in a relative you all hold in common. For example in order to generate interest in the 125th anniversary of my grandfather's coming to America, I would say, "Come and celebrate I. I. Ottem 125th anniversary of his immigration to the New World – 1880 - 2005." Each of the people invited would be a direct descendant of his. I might include his picture on the invitation and entitle it "I. I. Ottem wants you to celebrate 125 years of new world living."

2. If you are pulling together a photographic display, let family members know that there will be a "premier showing" of photographs they won't want to miss. Tease family that you might use some bare-bottom baby pictures.

3. You may also want to let relatives know that your ancestor's old writing desk or the iron that he used to brand horses will be on display.

4. Or you may ask a few questions on the invitation to test people's knowledge of family history such as: How many siblings did your grandfather have? How much did he pay for his first team of oxen? Come to the reunion and find out.

5. A cookbook can create interest in a family reunion. Have families submit recipes for the book. Especially if a recipe of your ancestors is available, highlight that recipe and say, "Come and get Myrtle Crago's famous Lemon Pie recipe. It will make the trip worthwhile."

6. Whether you try photographs or displays or a recipe book to entice people to leave their busy lives, most people are pleased that they made

the effort to come to a family reunion – especially if such an event is well done.

FINDING RELATIVES

Plan sufficient time to locate relatives. Any reunion begins with a well-researched list of relatives. Start with the ones you have and ask them to give you names, addresses, phone numbers, and e-mail addresses of others. Find a contact person from each family grouping. To save time, fill in an ancestral chart as you go. You may be surprised how quickly you can find the missing links. However, start early so you will have plenty of time to contact relatives and inform them of the date. You may want to start your search one to three years before the reunion just to give yourself time to enjoy the process. Always ask for an e-mail address. Store it in your e-mail address book for future reference. Imagine the savings on postage alone, and you can gather information quickly.

You can use telephone directories (often public libraries have these directories on the shelves) to find phone numbers and address information. With a few phone calls you might be able to find any missing information. You may need to call directory assistance to obtain some addresses, but go lightly. All too soon you can have a very high phone bill, especially if you have chatty relatives.

Collecting relative information can be fun. Keep any information about family groupings in either a notebook with pockets or a set of manila folders. You will want to have this information available when you compile ancestral charts or the family history book. All the effort you put into obtaining addresses is well worth it. Nothing is worse that planning an event and having no one come. A complete database of names and addresses is key to that success. While you are obtaining this information, you will also find out other interesting facts about your family. You may be the one who is privy to some family secrets. With word processing and labeling, you can easily input the data once and have it available for successive mailings.

105

THE WEB SITE

Consider setting up a family website to help people keep in touch. Find someone who is a techy to do this work. And don't forget to praise the one who is willing to handle the Internet access.

THE INVITATION

Plan to create an enticing invitation. Once you have gathered up a complete and accurate address list, you will want to design an invitation. Make it inviting and colorful. Include the place, dates, and contact person on the invitation. If there is a charge, that fee should be included. You may also want to include lists of hotels and maps for out-of-town family. Make sure you have folks RSVP by a certain date so you can plan more accurately. Don't forget to solicit help for this big undertaking. Have them volunteer to work on one of the following:

_____ program
_____ history book
_____ children's activities
_____ photography or video recording
_____ set-up
_____ clean up
_____ food
_____ music or other entertainment

THE LOCATION

You will need to select a location for the reunion. Although choosing a location closest to most relatives is wise, you may also want to try other locations. Think about having a reunion in a foreign country where your ancestors came from, or have the gathering on or near the farm or home where your common ancestor lived. If the farmstead remains in the family, it would be a great location. If a granary could be used for the occasion, you have a perfect shelter and plenty of room for the program, dance, and flea market. Maybe some relatives could be enticed into coming if they could bring their crafts, books, or antiques, and offer them for sale. If pets are welcome, consider sites that allow animals.

Sometimes the best place for a reunion is a recreational facility where there are swimming pools and other playground equipment for children and those who want physical activity. Nearby mountain hiking trails may be an adequate reason for some to come to a family reunion.

After you determine the number of people you think might attend, don't forget to think about these concerns in selecting a place to meet:

1. Washrooms
2. If it is an outdoors facility, a shelter in case of a rainstorm.
3. Tables and chairs
4. Ability to reach the facility for those who are handicapped.
5. Parking for vehicles and recreational vehicles
6. Insect and bug control
7. Lighting for an evening meeting.
8. Hotel or motel facilities
9. Entertainment for children
10. Meeting hall
11. Amplification system
12. Entertainment
13. Food

Think about YMCA camps, or a municipal, state or national park. Sometimes church camps offer inexpensive facilities for large groups during off-season times. Sometimes such places close for the 4th of July week, and you might be able to host your family reunion then. Local city or county or state parks often have shelters that make for great get-togethers. Civic organizations such as the Elks or American Legion may have facilities available for rental and certain hotels will accommodate in providing space for a family gathering. Maybe a large hotel could cut a deal on the rooms if you agree to hold your reunion there. If you have your reunion at a camp, you might not even have to worry about meals. Often times those can be included in the arrangements, and you can forget your worries about feeding the group that gathers. However. . .

FOOD

Plan ahead for food. Food can be one of the most difficult parts of the reunion. It can also be the most fun. First determine how many meals will be needed. If the reunion consists of one meal, you may want to have it catered or have a potluck. If you are going to have a potluck, you may want to assign all people with *first names* A – K to bring a salad, L - Q to bring a dessert, and R - Z to bring a main dish. That will allow for a variety. And you can ask everyone to bring extra recipes of their food just in case anyone is interested in trying that dish out at home. Ask everyone to bring their own picnic plates, cups, and eating utensils. It cuts down on garbage, and eliminates the need to wash dishes.

The reunion committee could provide the coffee, cool drinks, and extra plates, cups, and eating utensils. You may want to ask for cash donations for the food and have someone grill hot dogs or hamburgers or arrange to have a pig roast. These make great family meals as well. If you are from Iowa you may want to have a corn festival and purchase corn from one of the local farmers.

It's great to have a lot of food. Ask people to bring a little more than what they would normally cook to feed their own family. Out of town guests can bring non-perishables such as the catsup, mustard, coffee, pickles, mayonnaise, etc.

THE PROGRAM

Plan an interesting program. A program can give structure to the event, and it just may be the highlight of any reunion. However, programs don't come together without significant planning. Here are some ideas for a successful one:

Family Archaeology

1. Master of Ceremonies. Find someone to serve as spokesperson for the event. When making the selection choose someone who has a strong voice and won't bore the relatives. Encourage the Master of Ceremonies to have a few clean jokes on hand.

2. Music. If you have musicians in your family, invite them to take part in the program. Portable keyboards, drums, and guitars can be transported. You can also hook up a sound system and have background music playing. However, there is nothing quite as good as live music. Family members may enjoy a sing-along. Karaoke has become popular as a means of entertainment, and even family members who can't sing will make a hit simply by trying. Choose favorite family songs. If you are Irish, try *O Danny Boy* or *When Irish Eyes are smiling.*

3. Family Leaders. A leader from each family grouping could be given the responsibility of organizing a family skit or dramatic reading or simply a report on happenings within their family. They could show pictures or slides of family members. "Then and now" always make for interesting conversation. Start with the common ancestor of that family grouping and then move on from there. Keep these presentations to about fifteen minutes.

4. Dance. The family could hire a live band, or encourage family musicians to play. If those aren't possible, contact a DJ for an evening dance or party. Be sure to include line dances where no partners are needed.

5. Religious Services. Often times a pastor can be contacted to hold a "family service," if you don't interfere with their regular church schedule. Services of this nature should be ecumenical. Choose music that is familiar to most. Christian services could use such favorites hymns as *Amazing Grace, How Great Thou Art, and What a Friend We Have in Jesus.*

6. Printed Programs. If possible, arrange to have a printed program available. People appreciate receiving something in writing. A short history of an ancestor could be included on the back of the program, and the front of the program could include a picture of the common ancestor or ancestors.

7. Memory Board. You may want to have a tri-fold board available for family members to leave memory messages about loved ones who have died. For example: *"Wish Mom could be here to see her grandchildren playing in the mud."*

8. Auction. Auction of family items could prove interesting. Maybe the family has a special charity. Designate an auctioneer and enjoy raising the money.

10. Family Sites Visits. If the location permits, you may want to schedule visits to family places, such as homes, churches, schools, and cemeteries.

11. Contests. Why not break out in laughter? Sponsor a "Calling the cows home" contest. Make sure the crowd cheers them on. You may enjoy having a corn-on-the cob-eating contest too. Look out for those teenage boys.

CHILDREN'S ENTERTAINMENT.

Plan for bored children. You may want to have a special committee that organizes activities for the children to do while grown-ups talk about their ancestors and the good old days. Advanced planning in this area will make the reunion much more pleasant. Here are some ways to entertain the children: (1) Rent a clown to make balloons (2) Have a horse or a pony available for rides. (3) Arrange a trip to an amusement park or even the local swimming pool. (4) Make computer or board games available. Ask a chess player in the family to challenge the kids and play five rounds at the same time. (5) Hire a puppeteer for a show. Or have the children make puppets of ancestors and then put on a show for the adults. (6) Take the kids to a movie or rent a video for them to watch. (7) Race with gunnysacks. Give medals to the winners. (8) Ask teenage girls to do face painting. Make sure you have the paints and brushes available.

Look for other resources in your local library or ask the leader of a 4-H club or Boy or Girls Scout troop for ideas. The kids might even enjoy a campfire in the evening with the adults. Marshmallow roasting is always fun, even for grown-ups.

THE HISTORY BOOK.

Plan ahead to preserve family history. Each family needs an historian. This person receives family records and has access to copying services so that pictures, copies of vital statistics, (birth, death and wedding, etc) histories, news clippings, and obituaries can be made available for all members of the family.

It's important to begin the book with the history of the common ancestor. Then include a chapter on each family grouping. Each child of the common ancestor would be considered a family grouping. Select a member of each family grouping to be responsible for gathering that information and submitting it to the historian. One or two others should work with the historian in compiling the information and editing it for accuracy. A book of this kind will be the most treasured information that the relatives receive. But don't make the historian angry. Rather than criticizing the typographical errors or the wrong birth date, make notes so that future additions include those corrections.

You may want to make up a history book after the reunion. This would give you an opportunity to gather additional information at the reunion, and include photos from that gathering in the book. Ask people to leave a check to cover printing costs.

THE PHOTOGRAPHS.

Hire a photographer or designate several people as photographers for the event.. If you have a professional photographer close-by, such a person may be willing to set up shop and take photographs of the whole family and each family grouping. Just as most people would not let a wedding pass without a professional photographer on hand, do what you can to make arrangements for a pro to attend. Some photographers have digital cameras and can make photos on the scene. For a nominal price, each person can walk away with professional photographs at the end of the reunion. Whatever you decide, photographs, informal and formal, become the lasting memory of such a gathering.

THE VIDEO RECORDER.

If someone has a video recorder, have that person make a tape of the event and offer copies of the video to interested parties. Remember to collect the money at the reunion. They could also interview people and ask them some basic facts such as:

1. Name (ask the women their full names)
2. Address (include where they grew up) Include e-mail
3. Names of their parents, grandparents, and great-grandparents. Also the names of their siblings and their children
4. What brought them to the reunion
5. What they have enjoyed most about being at the family gathering

Margaret Mead said, "*No matter how many communes anybody invents, the family always creeps back.*" Celebrate your family. Hold a family reunion.

POSTSCRIPT

———

S oren Kierkegaard said, *"Life can only be understood backwards; but it must be lived forwards."*

Our families give us a unique window to our past. May those ancestors peering from solemn black and white photos captivate your attention. They are your kindred folk. There may be a part of them calling you to a new bold venture. Listen.

ABOUT THE AUTHOR

FREYA OTTEM HANSON lives in the Twin Cities of Minnesota, with her husband and teenage son. She enjoys playing her grand piano and taking walks with friends. *FAMILY ARCHAEOLOGY: Discovering the Family Skeleton and Making it Dance* is the first in a series of titles that give practical ways to recapture family stories and traditions and reshape them for a new generation. Freya grew up in Osnabrock, North Dakota, holds a BA degree from Concordia College, Moorhead, and a law degree from William Mitchell College of Law, St. Paul, Minnesota. She is the author of several books including *The Scopes' Trial*, *The Second Amendment*, and *Just a Soldier*, the latter a memoir collection of her father's World War II letters.

www.ingramcontent.com/pod-product-compliance
Lightning Source LLC
Chambersburg PA
CBHW071228290326
41931CB00037B/2451